THE MIRACLES
OF
CHAIRMAN MAO

A compendium of devotional literature
1966 - 1970

Edited and introduced by
GEORGE URBAN

Nash Publishing • Los Angeles

Published by arrangement with Tom Stacey Limited,
28 Maiden Lane, London WC2E 7JP England.

Copyright © 1971 by George Urban

Library of Congress Catalog Card Number: 79-186894
Standard Book Number: 8402-1246-1

First British Commonwealth edition: 1971.
Published in the United States of America in
1972 by Nash Publishing Corporation, 9255 Sunset
Boulevard, Los Angeles, California 90069.

Printed in the United States of America.

First Printing

Acknowledgements

I am indebted to Mr. Joseph C. Kun for scholarly advice generously given, and I am especially grateful to Miss Margaret Evling for helping me to edit and proof-read the texts.

Editor

Note

In accordance with current Chinese practice, quotations from the writings of Mao Tse-tung have been printed in bold and between quotation marks.

As the majority of texts used in this selection comes from the English-language organs of the Chinese Party and Government, no improvements have been made in the English except where imprecision or some linguistic infelicity demanded clarifications. These, however, have been kept to a minimum.

Words and phrases which are peculiar to the current phase of Maoism and are not explained by the context in which they occur, are listed and explained in the Glossary.

Story titles which are printed in quotation marks are the original titles or have been taken from the original texts. All other titles are those of the editor.

Contents

Introduction   *xi*

CHAPTER I   *Miracles*
"How we removed a 45 kg. tumour" .   .   1
Fighting cancer with revolutionary optimism   9
Deaf-mutes   13
Restoring sight   21
"Chairman Mao has given me a second right
     hand"   23
Resurrecting the dead   .   .   .   24

CHAPTER II   *The power of faith*
Pursuing the tottering foe with
     Chairman Mao's poem .   .   .   28
Faith driver   29
Faith flyer   29
Faith sailors   29
Faith players   30
Faith saving   37
Braving the tunnel   .   .   .   40
Turning the tide   41
Spiritual atom-bomb aids harvest   .   43
Cancer is a paper tiger   .   .   .   44
Operating with sewing needles .   .   45
Observation of solar eclipse defeats
     imperialism   46
Fishing for the revolution .   .   .   47
Wiping out snails   48

CHAPTER III   *Abnegation of self*
Night-soil collectors   49
Surrendering manure inspires poem   .   49
Purging self with castor beans   .   .   51
Barefoot doctor's sacrifice .   .   .   52
"How can we be frostbitten?"   .   .   53
Stricken peasants refuse relief   .   .   54
Reluctant wives fall in line   .   .   55
"Children are precious wealth of the Party
     and people"   56
Model family   61
Cutting hair for the revolution .   .   64

CHAPTER IV   *Class love*
Class love overrides wife's death . . . 67
Closer than parents and children . . 71
A ladle of water 72
"If you need skin, strip it from our bodies" . 73
Class brothers 74
Doing good all one's life 75
Saving the patient for socialist construction . 75
Room at the inn 77

CHAPTER V   *Socialist sacrifice*
Death as a last affirmation of loyalty to
    Chairman Mao 81
"Five young pine trees" . . . 82
Dying for collective sheep . . . 83
A martyr's diary 85
Martyr posthumously received into the Party 94
"Sacrifice of the few is the cost of happiness
    for the many" 95
"If you want to know the taste of a pear" . 95
Self-effacing hero 97
Red women rouse seamen 98

CHAPTER VI   *Guilt and confession*
Reaching the depths of their souls . . 99
Vexed by unclean spirits 101
Baring one's self-interest 103
Recanting father 105
Reformed son shoulders burden . . 107
Exorcising expertise 109
Doctors' error 110

CHAPTER VII   *The frugal, the pure and the humble*
Frugal weddings 113
Patient groom 114
No dowry for Hsueh-chiao . . . 114
No new clothes for the bride . . . 118
"Sugar-coated bullets" 118
Humility in office 119
Thaumaturgic blacksmith . . . 120
Exalting the lowly 122
"Thank Chairman Mao" 123
Ascetic storekeeper 124
Cow-dung cures ideological disease . . 124

CHAPTER VIII *Spreading the word*
  Red bards 126
  Singing to a purpose 128
  Little red soldiers 129
  Tree-top broadcasters 131
  Every home should have one . . . 132
  "Whole family red" 133
  Street study 134
  Training 136
  Airborne with Chairman Mao . . . 137

CHAPTER IX *Loving Chairman Mao*
  Chairman Mao in his bodily reality . . 138
  Painting the "Red sun in our hearts" . 140
  The power of Chairman Mao's image . . 144
  The recitation of Chairman Mao's words . 150
  Obeying Chairman Mao 153
  Merging self with Chairman Mao . . 155
  The memorial meal 155
  Immortality and rebirth in Chairman Mao . 156
  Socialist pilgrimage 159
  The glorification of Chairman Mao . . 160

APPENDICES A. The "three constantly read articles":
      In memory of Norman Bethune . . . 165
      Serve the people 166
      The foolish old man who removed the mountains 168
    B. A Soviet view of the cult of Mao Tse-tung:
      The making of an idol by M. Yakovlev . 171

GLOSSARY 179

Introduction

Maoism is one of the wonders of ideological crossbreeding. Pure strains in ideology are, of course, always hard to come by; Marx and Engels were bourgeois Rhinelanders who settled in England. Their economic theories derived from, and were designed to cure, the ills of West European society then on its way to industrialization. Yet, in the hands of Lenin, they were first bent to the needs of an under-developed, agrarian Russia, and later further distorted to fit the Byzantine designs of Stalin. The results had a great deal to do with the autocracy which Leninism had replaced in Russia, but very little with what Marx and Engels had written about. Yet Lenin's and Stalin's sectarianism[1] strikes one as well within the "normal" tradition of European despotisms set against Mao Tse-tung's thought and the application of his philosophy in the cultural revolution.

Much ink and acrimony will be spent in deciphering the intellectual origins of Maoism: Marx and Lenin, Confucius and Mencius, silent assumptions about China's cultural superiority, Mao's nationalism and the xenophobia of his generation have all played their part. Whatever the mixture, the transplantation of a body of opinions from one socio-economic environment to another has always been a delicate operation. The history of religion abounds in examples. In the Maoist variety of communism the Marxist element had, inevitably, the roughest passage. Stalinism did not travel much better. Yet, the journey from Moscow to Peking has, in a sense, tempered the crudities of Stalin's legacy. Maoism, though equally thought-killing and intolerant, has shown itself to be still fresh with the excitement of revolution and hence closer to the concerns of hungry and under-housed men and women than Moscow's doctrine. The Soviet model, with its insipid conservatism and a proletariat well set on its way to *embourgeoisement*, has nothing to say to the under-developed world to which China belongs. China *has* and her relevance may not be entirely confined to the poorer nations.

What is her message? When the verbiage is peeled off and the appalling cruelties of the 1951-52 "three-anti" and "five-anti" campaigns (*see* Glossary) are placed in historic perspective (and putting

[1] 'Revisionism' would apply with almost equal justification, for in the unsettled heritage of Marx, heresies and orthodoxies are freely interchangeable, depending on who speaks from the pulpit.

them in perspective is not to excuse them), we are left with a handful of ethical imperatives. Maoism is a serious call to a socially responsible moral conduct which has a great deal in common with Christian rectitude, especially in its Protestant and Victorian embodiment. It stresses the social virtues of temperance, frugality, humility, sacrifice and hard work. It insists on man's ability to overcome nature, including his own, by a sheer assertion of will. It exalts the "socialist" organization (though it denies the hierarchy) of the family which serves as a microcosm of the state. Such values are in short supply in the West too. For those enjoying a sense of guilt about the surfeit and meretriciousness of our civilization, Maoism offers a beguiling guide for action.

Mao holds that the mortification of self is the first stage of revolution. This has already produced an effervescence in the student generation in Western Europe and America, even if in forms so distorted that they can hardly be said to be more than tangentially related to Mao's message.[1] It contains a yet more important factor. Although Maoism has scrupulously distanced itself from anarchism – and had very sound reasons for so doing in the light of the excesses of the cultural revolution – it advocates a continuously recurring social regeneration and places it at the heart of the cultural revolution. This rejuvenation of the sinews of society, Mao's war on bureaucracies and establishments of all kinds,[2] carry an emotional charge that makes them seem at least superficially relevant to the problems of sophisticated, industrialized societies. That Mao's message comes to us from an *étatism* which is not demonstrably less oppressive, and is certainly more de-personalizing, than the one it has ousted, is not appreciated in the West, or else it is discounted as the Party's over-reaction to Mao's iconoclasm.

But Mao's influence is paradoxical. If his stress on Confucian and, some would say, Christian moral values engages our sympathy, the way in which these values are applied and propagated evokes our repugnance. The saintly life is preached from an ant-heap. It invites emulation by social insects, not men. The ideal type of Maoist rectification is the fully conditioned moron who, by some

---

[1]"Make love not war" and "political power grows out of a barrel of a gun" make strange bedfellows, though Eldridge Cleaver's claim that "revolutionary power grows out of the lips of a pussy" offers a bizarre explanation of their juxtaposition.

[2]This, in the language of Chinese (and Far Eastern) history is simply breaking the "dynastic cycle" in which leading positions in the state hierarchy were hereditary, not elective. The cultural revolution may thus be seen as an antidote to the personal, psychological degeneration of a leadership which, having conquered power, has opted for a period of rest and consolidation.

freak, is both unquestioningly obedient to the Maoist ethic and capable of displaying superb feats of initiative. Can such clearly inhuman means serve ostensibly humane ends?

In the context of Chinese civilization the paradox is not as profound as it would appear to Western eyes. Filial piety (Hsiâo), respect for the rules of propriety (Li), the emulation of human models, a high sense of conformity in speech, dress and ceremony, a traditional trust in the malleability of the human material ("The people are born good, and are changed by external things", [1] *The Shu King*, Book XXI, third century B.C.), all prepared the ground for the acceptance of Maoism as China's substitute religion in an age of transition.

In a sense the cultural revolution itself is a typically Chinese rather than a Marxist phenomenon. No other communist country has had one; [2] but then communist countries are seldom run by poets. There is more than superficial connection between Chiang-ching's (Mme. Mao's) reform of the Peking opera and the dictum in *Yo Ki* (China's ancient *Record of Music*): "We must discriminate sounds in order to know the airs; and airs in order to know the music; and the music in order to know the character of the government". [3] One can trace, in the imagery and usages of Maoism, almost every detail back to the Chinese classics. For instance, the Maoists' predilection for casting their slogans in numbered categories (the "two-lines", the "three-capitulations and one abolition", the "four-olds", the "five-category elements", and so on, *see* Glossary) derives directly from the sacred books of China. Thus in *The Shu King* the "Great Plan" falls into "nine divisions"; we read of "eight objects of government", "the five punishments", "the five dividers of time", "the five personal matters", etc.

None of this is to pass moral judgement on the Chinese people's fitness to be treated as political adults. But it would be surely foolish to deny that while to a Frenchman, with 1789, Blanqui, Proudhon and the Paris Commune in his intellectual heritage, "rectification" would seem an insufferable insult to his intelligence, a modern Chin-

[1]According to a Western Han legend, often regarded as one of the foundation stones of Chinese education, Mencius's mother changed her domicile three times before her son began to show moral and intellectual improvement.

[2]China had. In 1898 the Emperor Kuang-hsü undertook to modernize China by sweeping cultural reforms. However, he was deposed by the Manchu Empress Dowager, Tz'u-hsi, his edicts were rescinded and he remained a prisoner for the rest of his life.

[3]Zhdanov had no such tradition to follow in Russian *culture*. His musical purism was based, much more clearly than the Chinese variety, on police power.

ese, heir as he is to centuries of conformism, emperor cult[1], and a hierarchic view of society, would react to demands for *cheng-feng* (mental remoulding) with greater tolerance and perhaps a sense of amusement and irony. Whatever its origins, in Mao's eyes "remoulding" is not an inhumane means, and it is even less inhumane by the yardstick of the Stalinist purges. It obviates the need for physical liquidation, diverting the Party's attention from the body to the mind of the object of rectification.

Given China's restricting cultural perimeters which have always set narrow limits to personal and intellectual freedom (well reflected in the cutting down of Chairman Mao's little flowers after the "contending and blooming" of 1956 and 1957),[2] Mao's particular method of conditioning the people may not, in itself, hamper the growth of industrialization and modernization but may, on the contrary, enhance it. (Whether industrialization and modernization are humane ends is another question). To us this may seem like an inordinate price to pay for a modicum of organization and comfort, but to a hungry country such as India, which is rapidly sinking into anarchy and is already ungovernable, the Maoist model may not be so repulsive.

It is to the ordinary, mostly illiterate and superstitious masses that the devotional literature which has built up around Mao Tse-tung is principally addressed. Mao is sophisticated enough to realize that although some learned treatise of his on the nature of contradicition or aesthetics will be willingly mouthed by the Chinese peasant if it is foisted upon him by authority, the charisma of Mao and the doctrine he represents will have no personal impact unless they are depicted in the kind of language Chinese peasants understand.

This requires adopting the mental attitudes and vocabulary of the parable, the proverb, the fairy story and the cautionary tale as they have come down in Chinese folklore and literature. Chairman Mao's "miracles", of which this book offers a modest selection, are

[1]Paying homage to "deified" leaders has been widely practiced even in modern China. The Nanking government set in train an official cult of Sun Yat-sen by ordering all government offices and schools to hold memorial sessions of Sun each Monday. These consisted of three bows before Dr. Sun's portrait, readings from Sun's will and the observance of three minutes' silence. Later a cult of Chiang Kai-shek was added. Whenever the names of Sun and Chiang appeared in print, they were elevated in the same way as were the names and canonized titles of emperors.

[2]Nevertheless the Chinese intellectuals could draw on a long line of historic precedents for believing that their criticisms were being honestly sought and that they would be acted upon. A time-honoured tradition of China ascribes to the intellectuals a duty to criticize the ruler. Confucius says that it is a minister's office to oppose his ruler to his face (*Analects*, 14.23). The "right of remonstrance", later institutionalized in the "Censorate", elevates, in fact, the scholar to the status of political critic.

all geared to some essential point in the Chinese Party's programme. Some support the extension of medical services to the rural areas, others demonstrate the feasibility of running hospitals and clinics without sophisticated personnel and medicines of which China is chronically short. But over and above that they evince the universal validity of Mao Tse-tung's philosophy. The message is simply that Maoism *is* a cure-all: *in hoc signo vinces*. The naive homilies, the endless labouring of moral points that are already painfully obvious, the chilling contrast between the good peasant and the wicked landlord, between the socialist masses and the "handful of capitalist roaders", between God (Mao) and the Devil (Liu) have a classical Chinese and also an Old Testament ring about them. Some of this material that pours forth from the (officially controlled) press and radio has a quality that endears by virtue of its sheer simplicity. Some of it attracts and amuses by its absurdity. But there are also items that assault our sense of natural justice. They assume that the individual has no intrinsic merit and deserves no respect unless he is a worker, a poor, or a lower-middle peasant, with two unpleasant corollaries; firstly, that those who are not members of this class are fair game for those who are and, secondly, that the state has a right to release the unconfessed springs of class-consciousness in those who belong to the chosen class but are insufficiently aware of it. This is the Marxist-Maoist doctrine of Original Virtue: custom, selfishness and remnants of bourgeois thinking may, for a time, suppress its call, but the state is there to help the sinner cleanse himself of these corrupting influences. Through contrition, confession and penance ("struggle, criticism, transformation" in the language of the cultural revolution) the class-deviant is "liberated" and restored to his natural role as an appointed maker of history. These are important elements in Maoism, yet its real significance lies elsewhere.

The voice of Mao Tse-tung is the voice of the church militant speaking with the reforming fanaticism and intolerance of a Savonarola. Mao's battle is for the soul of the world communist movement, and the restoration of China's power and self-respect is only the first step on that way. To a young and dedicated communist, especially if he is an African, a Latin American or Asian, Moscow's voice is unprophetic and heavy with the boredom of establishment. It is the voice of a sated giant whose economic targets are those of the United States and whose social and cultural values are daily growing more akin to those of the United States. Peking inspires because it speaks from poverty and because its avowed aim is (to adapt Macaulay) to make men perfect, not to make imperfect human beings comfortable.

It is true that the cultural revolution is about industrialization, about thought-reform, about a power struggle. But its full importance lies beyond. In the short run, the challenge of Maoism as it emerges from the upheavals of 1966-69 is a challenge to the Euro-centric tradition of the world communist movement and therefore also to the power and influence of the Soviet Union. For the first time in the history of communism the defiance of the Soviet Union has been written into a communist party's constitution.[1] In the long run, Maoism may furnish the non-white races of the world with a religion to rally the power implicit in their numerical superi-ority over the white races.

An aura of primitive religion pervades the extracts which follow. The legends being officially propagated cover the gamut of religious appeal from sacrifice and the sanctity of relics to the mystic union with the (still living) godhead. In China today a new hagiography is being seeded, appealing to the irrational in the name of a faith which claims exclusive commerce with a scientific understanding of history.

G R U
London, June 1970

---

[1] The 1969 Constitution of the Chinese Communist Party.

THE MIRACLES OF
CHAIRMAN MAO

If there were a true king upon the throne of China, unquestionably Manhood-at-its-best would prevail within one generation.

Confucius

Chapter 1

Miracles

"HOW WE REMOVED A 45 kg. TUMOUR"

. . . In February, a railwayman, Tsui Ping-wu, brought his ailing wife Chang Chiu-chu in a pushcart to our health section. As soon as he caught sight of us he came up and tightly grasping our hands as though we were his closest kin said: "P.L.A. comrades, I have brought you a patient who is waiting to die!" Then we saw that Chang Chiu-chu was kneeling in the cart painfully supporting herself with her two arms. Her abdomen was swollen to a frightful size. She couldn't reach her navel with her hands, and she breathed with difficulty.

Seeing such distress in a sister of the labouring people, our deep proletarian sentiments were stirred. We examined her immediately and discovered that a huge tumour filled her abdomen and half her chest. Although she was thin, she weighed as much as 96 kg. We had never seen, or even heard of, such a patient before. What should we do if we agreed to take her in?

The railwayman went on to tell us something of their quest for treatment. "We discovered the trouble in 1964" he said, "and immediately took her to several big hospitals for treatment. But some bourgeois 'specialists' there diagnosed it as an 'incurable disease' and practically shoved her out of the hospital. So she got worse and worse, and her tumour, which was then only the size of a rice bowl, grew gradually to the size you now see it. She can't sit, stand or lie down, and day and night she kneels on the bed, completely unable to look after herself. Our whole family is broken-hearted. I know you are not a big

I

hospital, and you have no 'specialists' or 'authorities'. I have come to find P.L.A. comrades who are loyal to Chairman Mao's revolutionary line. Please take her in!"

His words were a scathing denunciation of the counter-revolutionary crimes of China's Khrushchev. They were a big education to us. We felt that what we confronted was not an ordinary case of treating a disease, but a sharp struggle between the two lines.

Chairman Mao teaches us: **"This question of 'for whom?' is fundamental; it is a question of principle"**.

In medical and health work, China's Khrushchev pushed the counter-revolutionary revisionist line of serving a handful of people in the cities. On the other hand, Chairman Mao has always called on us to serve the workers, peasants and soldiers, to serve the broad masses of the people. Therefore, to take Chang Chiu-chu in or not was a matter of whether or not we were loyal to Chairman Mao's revolutionary line.

When we reported the matter to the Party committee of our unit, it promptly gave us a clear-cut directive: "Small as are the doors of your health section, they must be thrown wide open to the poor and lower-middle peasants!" The Party branch in our section decided: We must not only take Chang Chiu-chu in, but we must do our best to cure her, our class sister!

Raising Our Level of Consciousness in the Struggle Between the Two Lines

The bourgeois reactionary line in medical and health work had passed the death sentence on Chang Chiu-chu for as long as four years. The patient had lost all hope, and resigned herself to wait for death. How could we help her build up confidence that her disease could be cured and have her co-operate with us in our treatment?

Discussing the matter, we came to the conclusion that only Mao Tse-tung's thought could help her gain this confidence. So we assigned medical orderly Li Wei-chao to study Chairman Mao's works with her.

The light of Mao Tse-tung's thought soon enlightened Chang Chiu-chu's mind. She realized she was a victim of the counter-revolutionary revisionist line of China's Khrushchev. She hung up a portrait of Chairman Mao above her bed and often said: "Chairman Mao! With your wise leadership, I am going to be saved!"

With her class consciousness and consciousness in the struggle between the two lines thus enhanced, she was not only confident of being cured, but also developed a revolutionary outlook on the question of life and death. She told her husband: "If by any chance I should die during the operation, you should still ask the P.L.A. comrades to take the tumour out and find ways to cure such things, so that they can do no more harm to us poor and lower-middle peasants". Thus she shed all fear about the operation. This was an important condition for it to proceed smoothly.

When we started to diagnose her disease, the first question that arose was: What sort of a tumour was it; was it possible to cure it completely?

Chairman Mao says: **"You can't solve a problem? Well, get down and investigate the present facts and its past history!"** We formed an "investigation group". This went the rounds of the hospitals which had previously examined Chang Chiu-chu or given her treatment. It brought back their original diagnosis that what she suffered from was a "retroperitoneal fibrosarcoma of low degree malignancy".

On hearing this, some of the comrades lost heart. The Party branch of the section realized that this reflected the poisonous effects of the revisionist line pushed by China's Khrushchev for a long time past in the medical and health field. So we opened a Mao Tse-tung's thought study class where, using Mao Tse-tung's thought as the weapon, we first of all criticized and repudiated the concept of "incurable diseases" . . .

Chairman Mao enjoins us to **"heal the sick and wounded and practise revolutionary humanitari-**

3

anism". The "authorities" and "specialists" who carried out the bourgeois reactionary line simply used "incurable diseases" as their excuse to wash their hands of the masses of the people. We revolutionary fighters who are loyal to Chairman Mao's revolutionary line are filled with deep proletarian sentiments towards the masses of the people; we will try to save every life and attend to all the wounded.

In the study class, we went on to criticize the idea of being afraid to take risks, which was actually a sign of standing on the bourgeois reactionary line and putting considerations of one's own interests, reputation or gain above everything else.

Through these studies, our level of consciousness in the struggle between the two lines was heightened, and our courage and determination grew. We made more than 30 different tests or check-ups on Chang Chiu-chu. Finally we boldly overthrew the original diagnosis and drew our own conclusion that hers was a benign tumour, not a malignant one. Later facts proved that this was precisely the case.

Trust and Rely on the Masses

Chairman Mao teaches us: **"The people, and the people alone, are the motive force in the making of world history"**, and **"We have always maintained that the revolution must rely on the masses of the people, on everybody's taking a hand, and have opposed relying merely on a few persons issuing orders"**.

China's Khrushchev and his agents have always advocated that it is necessary to rely on "technique" in the treatment of diseases and to follow the line of relying on "specialists". Chairman Mao's revolutionary line demands that we put politics in command of technique, resolutely trust and closely rely on the masses.

In the Mao Tse-tung's thought study class, we thoroughly criticized and repudiated China's Khrushchev's counter-revolutionary revisionist line and pledged to carry out Chairman Mao's revolutionary line effectively.

All the comrades in our section—doctors, medical orderlies, members of the mess squad, the wounded and the sick in the hospital—threw themselves into this battle. Everywhere people discussed ways to cure Chang Chiu-chu's disease. Many suggestions and measures were advanced which were finally summed up in ten points of how to deal with the case and in more than 120 concrete measures to be taken.

Our way was beset with all sorts of difficulties, but no difficulty can intimidate people armed with Mao Tsetung's thought. Take the question of anaesthesia. We didn't have an anaesthetist. Dr. Kao Chia-cheng had once taken lessons in administering anaesthetic, but for only three months. Now we assigned the task of giving Chang Chiu-chu anaesthetic to a group of three led by him. They repeatedly studied "the three constantly read articles"—Chairman Mao's *Serve the People, In Memory of Norman Bethune* and *The Foolish Old Man Who Removed the Mountains*—and considered the problems that might arise. They prepared three sets of anaesthetic apparatus, yet they still did not feel completely easy in their minds, so they prepared a locally improvised anaesthetic device before the operation started. It was through such united efforts and wisdom that in the end they worked out a fairly good plan for anaesthesia.

To remove such a big tumour, what kind of incision should be made so that the whole tumour could be removed with minimum damage to the surrounding normal tissue and a quick recovery assured to the patient? To solve this problem, medical orderly Feng Hsueh-ming spent three nights without sleep to draw eight incisions and revised them over 30 times. Finally, through the concerted efforts of all the members of our section, a satisfactory incision was worked out.

Like those in the health section, the cadres, the fighters, workers and staff, and family dependents in our barracks all went resolutely into action. We just had to say what we needed, and we immediately received enthusiastic support from all quarters. Backed by the united efforts of the masses, we successfully devised a satisfactory plan for the operation and prepared all the materials needed.

Using Mao Tse-tung's Thought to Direct The Battle

On the morning of March 23, the battle to defend Chairman Mao's revolutionary line was due to begin. The Party committee of our unit decided to send its deputy secretary and other leading comrades to personally direct our battle with Mao Tse-tung's thought as the weapon.

At 7.40 a.m., the eight fighting groups, including those charged with political guidance and the performance of the operation itself, took up their respective combat stations. The patient Chang Chiu-chu was brought into the operating room. On leaving her ward, she and medical orderly Li together recited several times this quotation from Chairman Mao: **"Be resolute, fear no sacrifice and surmount every difficulty to win victory"**. Without any misgiving, she lay composedly on the operating table.

Five minutes had hardly elapsed after the administering of anaesthetic than signs of danger appeared. Chang Chiu-chu breathed with great difficulty; her blood pressure dropped and her heart beat faster and faster. She broke into a cold sweat and her face turned blue. She seemed on the point of ceasing to breathe. At this crucial moment, the deputy secretary of the Party committee exhorted all present to follow Chairman Mao's teaching: **"What we need is an enthusiastic but calm state of mind and intense but orderly work"**. Inspired by the mighty force of Chairman Mao's words, the comrades gave the patient a calm and careful examination and traced down the cause of the trouble. Doctor Kao Chia-cheng boldly decided to replace the original anaesthetic apparatus with the locally improvised device. This proved effective, and the smooth performance of the operation was ensured.

When the actual surgery began, we came up against new difficulties. The tumour was covered by a membrane and we could not make out whether this was the membrane of the tumour or actually the peritoneum. If it was the latter, then we should protect it; otherwise, the viscera might be contaminated and our class sister's future health would be affected. The question of whether the operation should be carried out through the peritoneal cavity or retroperitoneally was also a struggle between Chairman Mao's revolutionary line and the bourgeois reactionary line. According to bourgeois and revisionist medical ideas, the operation would be regarded as successful so long as the tumour was removed and the patient did not die during the operation. Chairman Mao, however, has always taught us: **"Our duty is to hold ourselves responsible to the people. Every word, every act and every policy must conform to the people's interests"**. So we must not only enable this class sister to live on in good health, but also to continue to work for socialism. Working thus conscientiously, the surgeons finally succeeded in avoiding entering the peritoneal cavity by smoothly carrying out the whole operation retroperitoneally.

But how to remove the huge tumour itself? We applied to our work Chairman Mao's military thinking: **"Attack dispersed, isolated enemy forces first; attack concentrated, strong enemy forces later"** and **"encircle the enemy forces completely, strive to wipe them out thoroughly"**. All agreed that the tumour bed would not be exposed until the tumour had been dissected.

In separating the tumour from the surrounding structures, the doctors found that it was covered with numerous blood vessels in the form of spider webs. In order not to injure the neighbouring tissues and to avoid profuse bleeding, they used small gauze rolls

7

held in clamps to separate the adhesions bit by bit. Ligation of the blood vessels was carried out step by step as the dissection proceeded so as to avoid, as far as possible, massive haemorrhage. Even so, there was still a considerable loss of blood due to the large surface of the tumour and the great number of blood vessels. The patient's blood pressure dropped several times and her heart beat abnormally. The 5,000 c.c. of blood made ready for transfusion soon ran out. Hearing that more blood was needed, comrades waiting outside the operating theatre vied with each other to donate their blood. Carrying portraits of Chairman Mao and written pledges and beating gongs and drums, more than 100 fighters of a guard company hurried to the scene to donate their blood. Chou Pei-hua, leader of the mess squad, went straight to the blood donors' bed, ready for a blood transfusion. Seeing that there was a tiny scar on his arm which indicated that he had already donated blood, the doctor advised him not to give any more. But Chou Pei-hua said: "In the old society, my parents were forced to sell me because we could not make a living. It is Chairman Mao who emancipated my whole family and reunited us. Now that Chairman Mao asks us to save the life of a class sister, how can I not donate my blood?" In this way, 38 cadres and fighters transfused into Chang Chiu-chu's body 7,520 c.c. of their blood.

After more than a dozen hours of arduous work, the fighters boundlessly loyal to Chairman Mao's revolutionary line finally succeeded in wholly removing the 45-kg. tumour from Chang Chiu-chu's body.

After she regained consciousness, Chang Chiu-chu was extremely excited when she felt her abdomen. The very first few words she uttered were: "Long live Chairman Mao! Chairman Mao has saved me!" Mao Tse-tung's thought gave her boundless strength and vitality. This was a major operation she had undergone, but she recovered quickly. On the sixth day, the stitches on the 95c.m. long incision were removed, and on the eighth day she could walk around. Now fit as a fiddle, she can do household work and farm labour . . .

Peking Review, No. 33, 16 August 1968

FIGHTING CANCER WITH REVOLUTIONARY OPTIMISM

. . . Hung Ping-chung, a technician of the Sinkiang bureau of the Civil Aviation Administration of China, was found to have cancer of the neck in December 1964.

"I was sent to a hospital in Peking with a cancer so big that the food I managed to swallow often went down my wind pipe. I was afraid that if the cancer kept growing I would die of starvation.

"I was given radiotherapy. With warm class feeling, the doctors and nurses showed great concern for me and advised me to study and apply Chairman Mao's works to the problem of my illness. They prepared any food I might fancy to get me to eat and the nurses wheeled me to see movies in the hospital.

"Although the comrades tried to comfort me and would not say I had cancer, I sensed that this was my ailment. Influenced by the philosophy of survival of China's Khrushchev and the descriptions of cancer by bourgeois reactionary academic authorities, I was in despair and waited to die.

"At that time, this instruction of Vice Chairman Lin Piao was made known: Chairman Mao's words are of the highest level, of the highest authority, and are most powerful. Every sentence of Chairman Mao's is truth, and carries more weight than 10,000 other sentences.

"I repeatedly studied Chairman Mao's three constantly read articles time and again so as to view the question of life and death properly. Sometimes I would

9

spend half a day reading, now and then lying down to rest a little. I reflected as I studied.

"I thought over these points made by Chairman Mao: **'All men must die, but death can vary in its significance. To die for the people is weightier than Mount Tai, but to work for the fascists and die for the exploiters and oppressors is lighter than a feather, and wherever there is struggle there is sacrifice, and death is a common occurrence. But we have the interests of the people and the sufferings of the great majority at heart, and when we die for the people it is a worthy death'.**

"I understand that a proletarian revolutionary fighter lives for the interests of the people and dies for the interests of the people. In facing life or death what he considers is public interest and not his own interest.

"I saw it was wrong to be pessimistic and I decided to fight back with an unflinching proletarian revolutionary spirit and live for the interest of the people. The more I studied Chairman Mao's teachings, the clearer my mind became. Chairman Mao's teachings gave me breadth of vision and released me from my spiritual fetters. I actively cooperated with the doctors in receiving medical treatment and met the challenge of cancer in the spirit of daring to struggle and to win.

"The radiotherapy affected healthy tissue in my throat and palate. Later my teeth came loose in the gums. It was agony to eat, even to swallow a mouthful of water. Radiotherapy also made me nauseous and I often vomited. I had to struggle with myself to eat every meal. When the pain was beyond endurance I thought I would rather die than live on in such agony; better not to force myself to eat and just give up.

"Whenever I had such thoughts Chairman Mao gave me fresh courage and strength. I felt that Chairman Mao was guiding me in my battle. Each time I vomited, I would force down another morsel. Sometimes it would take me two hours to eat my meals.

"After four months of radiotherapy and three months

of recuperation I was fit enough to resume my work. But some months later, in January 1966, cancer was found in the right lower side of my abdomen. When my comrades learned this, some wept. Many leading cadres visited me in the hospital. Their great care and attention made me feel that my disease had reached a very serious stage. I remembered the class brother who died in a Peking hospital, and the earlier prediction of bourgeois reactionary academic authorities that if a cancer moved from one part of the patient's body to another he would certainly die.

"This set my mind in turmoil. Although I had decided to live for the people and die for the people, Mao Tsetung's thought had not taken deep root in my mind. Personal considerations again crept in and made me lose confidence.

"I again turned to Chairman Mao's three constantly read articles, every word of which shines like gold. I studied the passages on life and death and his teachings that revolutionaries should be wholly dedicated to the liberation of the people and work entirely in the people's interest.

"One must go through many tests in order to look at life and death like a thorough-going proletarian revolutionary. In these tests there are bound to be repeated struggles between public and private interest and between Mao Tse-tung's thought and bourgeois ideology. In order to overcome bourgeois ideology one must be boundlessly loyal to Chairman Mao, Mao Tse-tung's thought, and his proletarian revolutionary line.

"Only when one reaches this ideological level can one, even if faced with death, think only of Chairman Mao and the revolutionary people in China and the world and not of oneself, like such heroes as Chang Tzu-te, Norman Bethune, and many others who dedicated themselves to the revolutionary cause.

"My experience taught me that without Mao Tse-tung's thought one would lose one's bearings. Ever since then I have studied Chairman Mao's works like a hungry person who seizes food.

"I was given a six and a half hour operation during which three malignant tumours which had nearly obstructed my intestine were removed. When I regained consciousness I felt an acute pain in my abdomen. At this time the image of Chairman Mao, serious, honest, and kindly, appeared before my mind's eye and filled me with warmth, and I seemed to hear his words: **'In times of difficulty we must not lose sight of our achievements, must see the bright future and must pluck up our courage'**.

"Radiotherapy was applied as a postoperative measure, and I acted in accordance with these teachings of Chairman Mao: **'Since you are here, you'd better relax. Don't in any way get impatient, but let your body gradually develop resistance to the disease until you finally conquer it. And when you do anything unless you understand its actual circumstances, its nature, and its relation to other things, you will not know the laws governing it or know how to do it, or be able to do it well'**.

"I learnt about cancer and tried to find the laws of change in my physical condition so as to move from the defensive to the offensive in my battle against cancer. I studied, when I had discomfort in my abdomen because of the disease, whether it was caused by changes in the weather, temperature, diet, or lack of rest. I also studied what kind of physical exercise was best suited to me.

"Within a month I discovered the laws. Most of my physical discomfort was due to changes in the environment and not to fluctuations in my health.

"This enabled me to fight on with revolutionary optimism. My health has steadily improved. Now I can play basketball steadily for 40 minutes. Every morning I run 3,000 metres. When I feel tired I shout: 'Long live Chairman Mao!' and 'Be resolute, fear no sacrifice, and surmount every difficulty to win victory'.

"My weight was only 45.5 kilograms when I came out of the hospital. Now it has reached 65 kilograms. I now move aeroplane parts each weighing 40 kilograms without great effort.

"Ever since June 1966 I have been working eight hours a day and sometimes work extra hours. But my energy has steadily increased . . .

"Chairman Mao has given me immense strength and taught me the correct relationship between personal life and the revolutionary cause, and what a proletarian outlook toward life and death is.

"Mao Tse-tung's thought has given me a second life. Moreover it enabled me to win victory in the struggle between proletarian and bourgeois ideology, and between Chairman Mao's proletarian revolutionary line and the bourgeois reactionary line of China's Khrushchev".

Peking Radio, 13 September 1968

DEAF-MUTES

To describe the impossible, people in China often used the saying "The dumb will speak only when the iron tree flowers". Today, with the light of Mao Tse-tung's thought shining over the land, many things formerly considered impossible have become possible. Miracles are being performed.

Inspiring news has recently come from Kirin Province. Relying on the invincible thought of Mao Tse-tung, a Mao Tse-tung's thought propaganda team of medical workers from the P.L.A. 3016 Unit's health section stationed in the Liaoyuan School for Deaf-Mutes has, by acupuncture treatment, enabled many of its mute students to speak. 129 of the school's 168 students can now hear, and 125 can cheer "Long live Chairman Mao!" "We wish Chairman Mao a long, long life!" 47 can sing *The East is Red* and other songs propagating

Mao Tse-tung's thought.

This is a great victory of Mao Tse-tung's thought; a rich fruit of the great proletarian cultural revolution.

Once-Silent Deaf-Mute School Rings With Joy

Over half a year ago, unbroken silence reigned in this school from morning to night. Students could only communicate with each other by finger signs or at best utter a few broken sounds that could not express what they meant. Today, both the classrooms and sports grounds ring with day-long laughter and chatter. Cheers of "Long live Chairman Mao!" and "We wish Chairman Mao a long, long life!" are heard, as are voices singing *The East is Red* and many songs of Chairman Mao's quotations set to music.

A Mao Tse-tung's thought propaganda troupe of 35 formerly deaf-mute students has taken 22 songs and recitations which they themselves composed to factories, mines, P.L.A. units and villages to spread Mao Tse-tung's thought among the workers, peasants and soldiers. They have everywhere evoked a strong response and been most warmly welcomed by the masses.

In early May this year, the troupe went by invitation to the Liaoyuan Mining Administration Bureau. When the curtain lifted, a miner's daughter Wang Ya-chin, who had been deaf and dumb for 17 years, appeared on the stage as master of ceremonies. In a clear voice charged with emotion, she began: "The 1000-year-old iron tree has flowered! The vines, withered for 10,000 years, have again borne fruit! Now, even deaf-mutes can speak, all because of our dear Chairman Mao . . ." Before she could say anything more, the whole hall burst into hearty cheers, and shouts of "Long live Chairman Mao!" rang out lustily for a long time.

When the performance ended, several old miners ran up the stage and hugged the young performers. Rumpling their hair, they said: "Dear children, in the old society, even if we poor people could speak, we had no voice! In the new society, deaf-mutes who could not speak can now talk. This has all been brought about by Chairman Mao!"

The "Forbidden Zone" Must Be Opened Up

In March this year, the health section of the 3016 Unit, implementing Chairman Mao's series of instructions on health work, formed a Mao Tse-tung's thought propaganda team of medical workers to go to the deaf-mute school to propagate Mao Tse-tung's thought and give the students acupuncture treatment at the same time. The team was made up of three army doctors and five medical orderlies. None of them had ever attended a medical school. Seven of them had only a primary school level. Only one had, for a short time, attended junior middle school.

When the propaganda team arrived at the deaf-mute school, the students were overjoyed. They took the hands of the P.L.A. men and waved them back and forth before a portrait of Chairman Mao in token of shouting "Long live Chairman Mao! A long, long life to him!" When the parents heard the happy news, they too told each other excitedly: "Chairman Mao has sent beloved P.L.A. men to treat our children!"

Seeing this, the propaganda team comrades were deeply moved. They stood before the portrait of Chairman Mao and took a solemn oath to cure these deaf-mute students.

News that the propaganda team was treating the students with acupuncture shook the so-called "noted doctors" and "specialists". They commented: "Who has ever seen anything in foreign medical books about treating deaf-mutes? It's preposterous to think you can cure them with a few needles!" "These raw soldier boys, what do they know? How can they cure deaf-mutes!" These derisive remarks roused the deep anger of the fighters. They drew strength from Chairman Mao's teaching: **"We the Chinese nation have the**

**spirit to fight the enemy to the last drop of our
blood, the determination to recover our lost
territory by our own efforts, and the ability to
stand on our own feet in the family of nations".**

The "noted doctors" and "specialists," the fighters
said in scorn, eat food grown by the people but do not
work for the people; they put blind faith in foreign
books and crawl behind others; they haven't in the
least got the spirit of the Chinese people! We are
determined to rely on the invincible thought of Mao
Tse-tung to open up a "forbidden zone": to cure
deaf-mutes with our shining needles!

The team investigated the case of each deaf-mute
child. They found that over 97 per cent of these children
were from families of workers or poor or lower-middle
peasants, in the old society, oppressed and exploited
by the landlords and capitalists . . .

The veteran worker Wang Yu-hai of the Liaoyuan
Mines, for instance, was badly exploited by the capitalists before liberation. He got married only after liberation, when he was already over 40. He had a daughter,
whom he named Wang Ya-chin. When a baby, she
fell sick, and because treatment was delayed, she became
a mute. Wang Yu-hai and his wife were full of hope
that well-known doctors in the hospitals could cure
their only daughter. But some "noted doctors" told
them, "Mutes are mutes. Even the foreigners can't
cure them, how can we!"

The worker Chang Chen-fang has a son, Chang
Li-ieng, who was also a mute. He took his child to a
big hospital where he sought the advice of a "noted
doctor". This man, with a reflector on his head, wagged
it back and forth in front of the child's ear and said
decidedly: "The ear drum is damaged. No amount of
treatment can cure him. Just forget it!" This old
worker came to the hospital with hope, but returned
home in tears.

Reading over the medical case histories of the children,
the comrades of the propaganda team were fired with

even stronger proletarian class feelings for the working people and deepened hatred for Liu Shao-chi. The fighters said: "These are not medical records, but indictments written in blood against Liu Shao-chi!" Turning their hate into strength, they were determined to relieve the sufferings of the deaf-mute students. On a wall they wrote up Chairman Mao's teachings: **"Serve the people whole heartedly"** and **"Be resolute, fear no sacrifice and surmount every difficulty to win victory"**. They kept these constantly in mind. They resolved to use the invincible thought of Mao Tse-tung to cure the "incurable".

Giving Treatment With Profound Proletarian Feelings

They first of all made repeated experiments in using the acupuncture needles on their own bodies. They tried the needles out on each other, and on themselves with the aid of a mirror. After the experiments, not a few of them had swollen necks or a ringing in their ears, or mouths so sore that they had difficulty taking food. But all this did not deter them. They were willing to take a thousand risks to win happiness for their class brothers. They vowed that they would not give the children any needle treatment of which they were not absolutely certain themselves.

The "*ya men* point" is an important point in the body for the acupuncture treatment of deaf-mutes. But "noted' bourgeois doctors and "experts" classified it as a "forbidden point". The old books on acupuncture also stipulated that at this point the needle should only be inserted to a depth of from 1 to 1.6 cms. But practice showed that insertion to this depth did not produce good results. Could they put the needle in any deeper? The "authorities" again chorused: If the needle is inserted to a depth of 3.3 cms., a healthy person becomes mute; insertion to a depth of 5 cms. endangers life.

Fully realizing the danger involved, the comrades

of the propaganda team braved it fearlessly. The medical orderly Chao Pu-yu was the first to experiment on himself. When he inserted the needle 3.3 cms. into the "*ya men* point", his nerves began to react, and he hesitated. What if the experiment really made me mute? he thought. As soon as he caught himself thinking this, he recalled Chairman Mao's shining words: **"Serve the people"**. Immediately he felt an onrush of fresh courage and silently made a resolution: In order to enable tens of thousands of deaf-mutes to cry "Long live Chairman Mao!", I would be willing even if I became mute myself. So he carried on without the slightest hesitation.

When the needle was inserted to a depth of 5 cms., he felt as if his head were swelling. To go in any further meant the danger of losing his life. Yet he bore in mind Chairman Mao's teaching: **"Wherever there is struggle there is sacrifice, and death is a common occurrence. But we have the interests of the people and the sufferings of the great majority at heart, and when we die for the people it is a worthy death"**. He carried on until he felt as if a wave of electricity was running through his head. This told him that he had found the most effective depth for treatment. It was only then that he pulled out the needle. When he measured it with his hand, he found that the depth of the insertion had been nearly 7 cms.

Through such repeated experiments, the comrades of the propaganda team mastered new techniques in acupuncture and acquired first-hand knowledge. They then used them widely on the deaf-mute students.

After a fortnight of treatment, they finally opened up a "forbidden zone": curing deaf-mutes! Of the 157 students under treatment, 70 were now able to hear distinctly and 32 out of the 70 could shout: "Long live Chairman Mao!" Chang Li-feng was the boy of whom the "noted doctors" and "specialists" had said, "the ear drum is damaged. No amount of treatment can cure him". Now he was also able to shout "Long live Chairman Mao!" for the first time in his life. Chien Shen-chi, who had been mute for 15 years, went home and in front of his whole family cheered: "Long live Chairman Mao!" They were so glad that they all shouted together, with tears of happiness, "Long live Chairman Mao! A long, long life to him!" When the neighbours heard this, they too hurried over to offer congratulations. Many people feelingly exclaimed: "These medical fighters armed with Mao Tse-tung's thought are really good!"

Enabling More Deaf-Mutes to Sing "The East Is Red"

One day, Fang Ying-teng, the responsible comrade of the propaganda team, discovered a girl student Wang Shu-fang, the daughter of a poor peasant, standing by the wall and wiping away her tears. This girl had already gained her hearing through their treatment, but could not yet speak. Fang Ying-teng asked her with deep concern what was the matter? The girl pointed to her mouth and then to other students, meaning that they could shout "Long live Chairman Mao!" and sing *The East Is Red*, but she couldn't, and she felt it keenly.

This set Fang Ying-teng thinking. Yes, he thought, the most deep-felt words the working people use to express their love for the great leader Chairman Mao are "Long live Chairman Mao! A long, long life to him!" The most resounding song they love to sing in praise of the great leader Chairman Mao is *The East Is Red*. As a medical worker of the people, it is my duty to do my best to help more deaf-mutes realize their fondest wish. Conscious of his responsibilities, Fang Ying-teng immediately examined Wang Shu-fang. It puzzled him that although the child had regained her hearing, which also opened up the possibility of speech, she was still unable to speak. He finally discovered that the frenum of her tongue was so thick and tightly stretched that her tongue could not move freely. This was the reason why she could not speak. This made Fang Ying-teng think of other students who were not able to speak, and he wondered if it was due to the same reason. Together with the comrades of the team, Fang examined in turn those students who could not speak even after the needle treatment. They found that 32 students suffered from the same disability.

The burning desire of the deaf-mute students to sing *The East Is Red* spurred on Fang Ying-teng to find a way to remedy the defect of their frenums. Late that same night, neglecting a high fever, he looked through many books on acupuncture and medical periodicals, but all of no avail. What should he do?

Remembering Chairman Mao's teaching that **"The masses are the real heroes",** he went, early the next morning, among the comrades of the propaganda team and called a meeting, asking each member to think up ways and means of tackling the problem. The fighters said: "What we can't find in the books, we can create in practice and write it into the books. We can break new paths untrodden by others". Everybody put forward suggestions and gave his opinions. After earnest discussions, they decided to repair the frenums by surgery. Having got the approval of the Party committee of the unit, the team made everything ready and performed the operation on the students. Every operation was successful. The girl student Wang Shu-fang was able to say clearly "Long live Chairman Mao!" the very next day after her operation.

*   *   *

The success of the P.L.A. 3016 Unit's Mao Tse-tung's thought propaganda team of medical workers in curing deaf-muteness proves once again that people armed with Mao Tse-tung's thought have the greatest combat effectiveness, and can surmount all difficulties and perform miracles.   Shih Liu and Szu Chi
Peking Review, No. 46, 15 November 1968

RESTORING SIGHT

. . . The left eye of Kao Fei-fu who came to the clinic had gone blind 29 years ago. Last year, his right eye, which had been diseased for 28 years, also went blind. He had gone to five big hospitals and the bourgeois "famous doctors" said: "There's a white membrane over your eyeballs. No matter how much we treat you, you'll go blind".

Although the members of the clinic had never treated the blind, they had profound proletarian feelings and made up their minds to see to it that their blind brother regained his sight.

The clinic had only one army doctor, one junior doctor, and two medical assistants. They had not studied ophthalmology, but they were determined to follow Chairman Mao's teachings and to obtain skill through practical experience. They decided to use new methods of acupuncture to treat the blind man. They experimented with the treatment on their own bodies.

The "*chingming*" point is important in treating cornea leukoma by acupuncture. The bourgeois "authorities" had stipulated: "Deep insertion is forbidden at this point". Books on acupuncture treatment said that the needle could only be inserted two fen.[1] Those who are proficient can insert the needle five fen, if necessary.

But medical assistant Liang Chin-hua, an activist in the living study and application of Mao Tse-tung thought and a Communist Party member, experimented on himself until the needle had been inserted to a depth of 18 fen. Ignoring the danger and carrying out repeated experiments, he finally gained the experience of inserting the needle deep in the area near the eye.

After being given this kind of acupuncture treatment several times, Kao Fei-fu's sight was restored. With tears in his eyes, he stood in front of a portrait of Chairman Mao, shouting over and over: "Long live Chairman Mao! A long, long life to him!"

[1] 1 fen equals about 0.33 cm.

Based on the experience obtained in the first case, comrades in the clinic restored the sight of more than 30 people whose blindness had been caused by leukoma. When the news spread, more and more patients went to this clinic, and cases were more complicated.

When treatment produced no effect on an old blind woman, the men of the clinic studied Chairman Mao's philosophical writings. In accordance with this teaching of Chairman Mao's: **"The principle of using different methods to resolve different contradictions is one which Marxist-Leninists must strictly observe".** They examined the patients one by one, made a general analysis, and found that this old woman was blinded by cataracts and only another method of treatment could help her.

Led by the battalion party committee, the comrades began trying to locate new points for acupuncture on themselves. For days on end, they tried needles of varying sizes and lengths in the area around their eyes using different manipulations. After months of trial efforts, they discovered six new points. By inserting needles in the new points they enabled the old woman to regain her sight.

In dealing with blindness due to cataracts, the comrades found that effects differed at the same points and when the same manipulation was used. To raise the therapeutic effect, they continued making tests on their own faces in the area near the eye and tried many different manipulations and made remarkable progress. In three months' time, they had treated 89 different types of cataract patients, and 90 per cent of them had made progress.

Witnessing this clinic's achievements in treating eye diseases, eye specialists from big hospitals and medical colleges and other visitors all praised the medical men, saying: "P.L.A. men armed with Mao Tse-tung thought can work wonders".

NCNA[1], 28 November 1969

[1] New China News Agency

"CHAIRMAN MAO HAS GIVEN ME A SECOND RIGHT HAND"

. . . Li Shu-fang, a worker in a farm tools plant in Liao-ning Province, had his right arm cut off near the shoulder while he was repairing some machinery. The severed arm was carried away by the driving belt and was itsel cut into two except for where the parts were joined by a tiny fragment of skin. The bones, muscles, nerves and blood vessels of the whole of the right arm were cut in two places. Li Shu-fang was rushed to the hospital, and on seeing him, the surgeons and nurses of the surgical department were determined to rejoin his severed arm and restore its functions by relying on invincible Mao Tse-tung thought.

They immediately formed an emergency team of cadres, surgeons and nurses. Comrade Kao Ching, a member of the hospital party committee and secretary of the party branch of the surgical department, joined the team in the battle to rejoin the severed arm and gave on-the-spot guidance.

Liang Chi-peng, a Communist Party member and deputy head of the surgical department, showed great concern over the patient's plight. He was calm and careful throughout the operation. After four hours' intense effort, he and his comrades overcame all the difficulties and successfully rejoined the upper arm.

With the upper arm rejoined, greater difficulty still lay ahead in the rejoining of the forearm which had now been detached for eight hours. According to all the literature on the subject, a severed limb cannot be revived after six hours. The patient had arrived at the hospital four hours after the accident, and the rejoining of the upper arm had taken another four hours. At this juncture, army doctor Li Chan-wen, a member of the Communist Party branch, got the team to study Chairman Mao's teaching: **"In times of difficulty we must not lose sight of our achievements, must see the bright future and must pluck up courage"**.

This boosted the medical workers' confidence and they resolved: "Since we don't have any previous experience to draw on, we must blaze our own trail. We are confident that we can succeed". They worked on perseveringly. Rejoining the forearm is more complicated, but men armed with Mao Tse-tung thought can work miracles. When suturing the blood vessels with a tiny needle and fine thread, every stitch must be perfect. One inaccurate stitch could make the operation a failure. Working in close coordination with the others, Liang Chi-peng, with a Red heart boundlessly loyal to our great leader Chairman Mao's proletarian revolutionary line, connected the radius artery, no bigger than a match tip, with 13 stitches extremely accurately placed. Blood circulation was restored. The operation was successfully concluded after nine hours of intense work.

Li Shu-fang's right arm was restored to use after five months' careful nursing on the part of comrades in the surgical department who directed their work with Mao Tse-tung thought. With profound emotion, Li Shu-fang wrote with his restored right hand the 11 Chinese characters: "Chairman Mao has given me a second right hand!" He raised his right arm and cheered: "Long live Chairman Mao!" Li Shu-fang has now returned to work.

NCNA, 4 November 1969

RESURRECTING THE DEAD

. . . On the cold afternoon of December 13, 1969, while fitting a steel bar on the roof of a three-storey building, a worker named Chou Te-ming received an electric shock. His body leaned back, and one end of the steel bar fell on a 6,600 volt high-tension wire. An old worker tried to haul Chou Te-ming away from the live wire.

He was thrown back by the force of the current, pulling Chou Te-ming away too.

Chou Te-ming was carried to the factory clinic for emergency treatment. His pupils were dilated, he was no longer breathing and his heart had stopped. These symptoms indicated that he was already in a state of clinical death. Artificial respiration failed, as did respiratory stimulants. His fellow workers rushed him by ambulance to the nearest hospital.

At 15.40 Chou Te-ming was carried into the emergency room of the Hsin-hua Hospital. His heart had stopped beating 18 minutes before he got there.

The doctor on duty felt it his responsibility to save this worker, but he recalled that according to a foreign medical journal, it was impossible for a patient to revive after the heart had stopped beating for six minutes. Could he save this worker after a much longer time?

Raising his head, he saw members of the workers and P.L.A. Mao Tse-tung's thought propaganda teams at his side. Their advice when they came to the hospital rang in his ears: "You must follow Chairman Mao Tse-tung's teaching, join the side of the workers, peasants and soldiers, and serve them whole-heartedly!" He must try to save Chou Te-ming!

The battle to save a class brother began with the workers and P.L.A. Mao Tse-tung's thought propaganda team at the command. On hearing of the case, medical workers of all the hospital's 11 departments went to the emergency room. The doctor on duty began cardiac massage, while the nurses undertook artificial respiration. But the patient did not respond, and seconds became minutes.

At that critical moment, the propaganda team read out quotations from Chairman Mao, urging them to **"Surmount every difficulty to win victory"**.

After a brief consultation, the medical workers decided to give the patient an injection of adrenalin, breaking with the foreign bourgeois conventions and old medical "text books" which rule out adrenalin in cases of electric shock because it causes strong contractions of the heart which may go into uncontrollable fluttering and result in death. The medical workers were prepared to use a defibrillator in that case, followed by cardiac massage after opening the chest.

Adrenalin was injected. At 15.45, 23 minutes after Chou Te-ming's heart had stopped beating, the heart began to throb. Five minutes later, the patient took his first breath. Chou Te-ming's life had been saved!

Mao Tse-tung's thought commands the battle

Chou Te-ming was still comatose, his breath'ng was abnormal and his limbs were in convulsion.

The critical question was whether his health could be completely restored since bourgeois "specialists" and "authorities" say that lack of oxygen to the brain for longer than seven or eight minutes causes irreversible damage to the brain cells, so that even if the patient's life is saved, he becomes an idiot. Now anoxia of the brain in Chou Te-ming's case had lasted longer than 23 minutes. Using Mao Tse-tung's thought as their guide in analysing this case, the medical workers were confident that if all necessary and effective measures were taken, they could save the patient. They broke with the old hospital conventions and took such measures as applying an ice cap and dehydration directly in the emergency room. Their actions lessened the degree and extent of swelling of the brain (cerebral edema), laying a good basis for further steps.

At the suggestion of the workers the Hsin-hua Hospital set up a "three-way combination" group composed of the workers, P.L.A. men and revolutionary medical workers to take charge of the case. This group rushed Chou Te-ming to the hospital affiliated to a military medical college in Shanghai because it has a high-pressure treatment room.

The Mao Tse-tung's thought propaganda team led all comrades in studying Chairman Mao's teaching on serving the people, taking as an example Doctor Norman Bethune who had boundless sense of responsibility in his work and boundless warm-heartedness towards all comrades and the people.

When the pressure in the high pressure room reached three atmospheres, Chou Te-ming's pupils started to dilate and his blood pressure dropped continuously. There was Cheyne-Stokes breathing, a sign of impending death.

The medical workers became tense. Members of the propaganda team reminded them of Chairman Mao's instruction: **"What we need is an enthusiastic but calm state of mind and intense but orderly work"**.

The doctors then calmly analysed the patient's condition and undertook heroic measures to deal with the principal contradiction, anoxia of the brain and cerebral edema. They were able to deal with the immediate crisis, and continued their work in the pressurized room for seven hours.

During that time, members of the propaganda team followed Chairman Mao's teaching: **"The revolutionary war is a war of the masses; it can be waged only by mobilizing the masses and relying on them"**. They asked other doctors and nurses to take part. With the joint efforts of the masses who were thus fully mobilized, Chou Te-ming began to take a turn for the better.

Chou Te-ming finally regained consciousness after 63 hours. 75 hours after his accident, he opened his eyes and clearly saw the portrait of our great leader Chairman Mao in his ward. His first words were: "Long live Chairman Mao! A long, long life to him!"

NCNA, 30 January 1969

Chapter II
The Power of Faith

PURSUING THE TOTTERING FOE WITH CHAIRMAN MAO'S POEM

. . . Both on the ground and in the air, from the flight command to the radar and telecommunications stations and the ground service units, commanders and fighters applied the invincible thought of Mao Tse-tung throughout the air battle. Ground commanders used Chairman Mao's quotations to give the following order: **"Go all out to wipe out the intruding enemies!"** and **"Be ruthless to our enemies!"** Hearing these words, Wang Chu-shu and Lu Chi-liang felt that the beloved great leader Chairman Mao himself was issuing the orders. Full of fight, Wang Chu-shu moved in on the enemy plane. Lu Chi-liang escorted him closely . . .

Wang Chu-shu's escort received his orders from the ground commander in the form of a line from one of Chairman Mao's poems: **"With power and to spare we must pursue the tottering foe"**. He opened fire and his first shot hit the reeling enemy plane which then exploded. From beginning to end, the air-battle lasted only a matter of seconds.

Wang Chu-shu and Lu Chi-liang have been nurtured by Mao Tse-tung's thought. In their daily lives, they follow Vice-Premier Lin Piao's instructions. . . . Therefore . . . they have become a "red pair" helping each other to overcome selfish thoughts. . . . In their cockpit hang portraits of Chairman Mao and quotations from Chairman Mao Tse-tung.

NCNA, 4 July 1967

FAITH DRIVER

. . . He got the engine running, put his toe on the accelerator while keeping the heel over the brake pedal, so that if he fainted or died he would automatically stop the lorry. Eyes blazing, he battled through the raging storm along the rugged muddy mountain road. Not only his shirt, but his arms and the steering wheel were spattered with blood. It was not the engine, but sheer will-power geared to the invincible thought of Mao Tse-tung that kept the lorry moving forward, up and down six slopes, across two streams, and round eight sharp bends. Liu Chih-chun finally reached a production team, where he fainted away as soon as he was given first aid.

People's Daily, 1 December 1967

FAITH FLYER

"One of our guides never fastened her seat belt; she told me that no safety precautions were necessary because the pilot could make no mistake, inspired as he was by Chairman Mao. The air hostesses even danced in the corridors of the aircraft, and on several occasions led communal singing of their favourite Maoist tunes. *Mao the helmsman* was a great favourite and very infectious at that".

Observer, 3 September 1967

FAITH SAILORS

. . . They pressed forward in the raging storm, but it was not long before a huge wave capsized their boat and threw them all into the sea. At this moment they kept

29

reciting Chairman Mao's great teaching: **"Be resolute, fear no sacrifice and surmount every difficulty to win victory"** to encourage each other.

They strove together to right the capsized boat, but the waves were too turbulent. After more than a dozen attempts, political instructor Wang Tien-chuan got the four of them together to seek ideas from Chairman Mao's teachings. All pledged themselves to stand up to the test of this life and death struggle.

Li Te-kuei, a fisherman with years of sea-going experience, promptly suggested that the mast and anchor be broken off to make it easier to turn the boat over. So they joined forces to break the mast off. They dived in turn, using the only knife they had to cut through the wooden holder to which the anchor was fastened. Eventually they managed to turn the boat over again . . .

NCNA, 13 August 1969

FAITH PLAYERS

What is the secret behind the rapid progress of the national Chinese table tennis team and its winning brilliant victories in international tournaments? The answer, members of the team say, is the great thought of Mao Tse-tung.

They drew this conclusion at a recent discussion in Peking when they reviewed their experience.

In the nation-wide movement to study and apply Chairman Mao's works in a living way, the world champion Chinese table tennis team has been both a pace-setter in sports circles and an outstanding example for the country as a whole.

An article written in 1960 by Chuang Chia-fu, a member of the team, was recently reprinted in many newspapers and magazines in China. He described how, during the 1959 world championships, Chinese table tennis players applied Chairman Mao's ideas on strategy and tactics and the principles contained in his articles *On Contradiction* and *On Practice.*

Since then, Chinese table tennis players have studied Chairman Mao's works more consciously and diligently and made great efforts to apply his ideas to remoulding themselves into thorough-going proletarian revolutionaries.

A series of articles written by Hsu Yin-sheng, Chuang Tse-tung, Cheng Min-chih and other outstanding players and Jung Kao-tang, Vice-Minister of the state commission of physical culture and sports, who led the Chinese team at the 1965 world championships, have won widespread attention as outstanding examples of their living study and application of Chairman Mao's works.

At the recent discussion, the Chinese players said that every victory and advance of the team had been achieved under the guidance of Mao Tse-tung's thought.

Chinese table tennis players learned from writings of Mao Tse-tung and from their own experience that sports and physical education contributed to and were a part of socialist construction and revolution. The playing of table tennis was a revolutionary endeavour and served the interests of the people. Like all others engaged in socialist revolution and construction, the players strive to reach the highest world levels.

Chinese table tennis players said that winning a match depended not only upon skill and tactics, but on the mental outlook of the player. When both sides had the same level of skill and tactics, the decisive factor was morale.

Their experience taught Chinese players that when they correctly understood and applied Mao Tse-tung's thought, they could show their skill to best advantage and give themselves the greatest possibility for victory.

They recalled that, inspired by the great leap forward in 1958, the Chinese players, like the rest of the Chinese people, have emancipated their minds by breaking with conservative thinking and shibboleths. The whole Chinese team at that time studied Chairman Mao's article *Problems of Strategy in China's Revolutionary War* and became better at making a dialectical analysis.

This enabled them to overcome their tendency to see the good points of the opponent more clearly than their own. This added to their confidence in scaling the heights of world table tennis.

At the 1959 world championships in Dortmund, Jung Kuo captured the men's singles title and China provided five semi-finalists in various events. This proved that the thinking of a player influenced his performance, in other words, how a confident outlook could be transformed into material strength.

The 26th world championships were held in Peking in 1961 when China was hit by natural calamities. In addition, the Soviet modern revisionists had withdrawn all their experts in a perfidious breach of contracts. But the Chinese players, like the workers of the Taching Oilfield, overcame the difficulties not by relying on foreign experts, but on the invincible thought of Mao Tse-tung. In a spirit of self-reliance, they overcame difficulties by hard work and intensive training to reach peak form for the championships. As a result they captured three championship titles—the Swaythling Cup, the men's singles and the women's singles—and were runners-up in four events.

A feature of the Chinese game at the 26th world championships was fearless attacking even under unfavourable circumstances.

During their pre-championship training, the Chinese players studied the fourth volume of the *Selected Works of Mao Tse-tung* just off the press at that time. They acquired from it a revolutionary spirit of daring to win and being skilful in struggle. They regarded this spirit as the guiding principle of their preparations for the championships. It helped them to break with the incorrect idea of regarding victory or defeat as a matter of personal gain or loss. They determined to be a credit to the team and show high morale even under unfavourable circumstances and against strong opponents.

Team coach Fu Chi-fang pointed out that in the all-out attacking game, the emphasis on speed, accuracy, power and variety of strokes evolved by the Chinese team was the application of dialectics to table tennis, in opposition to metaphysics and idealism. It was a result of study by the Chinese players of Mao Tse-tung's thought.

Fu Chi-fang said that the players recognized, after analysing the pattern of attacking strokes, that speed, accuracy, power and variety of strokes comprised the four different aspects of attack. Speed was the principal aspect of the contradiction, and any stroke intended to impart a spin to the ball must be executed without affecting the speed. The emphasis on speed, accuracy, power and variety of strokes represented an attempt by the Chinese players to arrive at a scientific generalization of the innate contradictions.

Hsu Yin-sheng, a member of the Chinese team, said: "Chairman Mao's teachings have enabled us to understand that we must set our own path to reach the top of the world. Looking back, it is now clear that for the past 10 years and more, we have followed a road of giving prominence to proletarian politics and Mao Tse-tung's thought".

That was why the Chinese players had been able to create a new style that combined speed, accuracy, power and variety of strokes. It was an example of how an ideological revolution brought about a technical revolution. Without the spirit of daring to explore and daring to excel, a new playing style could not have been created, and without the spirit of daring to fight and strive for victory, the new playing style could not have achieved the success it had.

At the closing of the 26th world championships, the Party had pointed out that the primary task was to pay attention to the fundamental question of raising the proletarian consciousness of the players, to ensure that Mao Tse-tung's thought was in command, foster proletarian ideology and eliminate bourgeois ideology, and prevent complacency.

It was pointed out by the Party that players should not only play well but, more important, should understand that their spare-time sport was part of the revolutionary cause, that in adopting the right approach to the game, they were preparing themselves to be proletarian revolutionary successors.

Acting in accordance with Chairman Mao's call never to forget class struggle, Chinese table tennis players took ideological remoulding as their basic preparation for the 27th world championships in Prague in 1963.

They joined the peasants in field work, joined servicemen in military training. They learned from the workers, peasants and soldiers, integrated themselves with them and developed the revolutionary tradition of arduous struggle. They regarded training and competition as a test in fostering proletarian ideology and eliminating bourgeois ideology, and turned every discussion of their summing-up into training in the living study and application of Mao Tse-tung's thought.

In this way they raised the level of their proletarian consciousness, eliminated the influence of bourgeois ideology and greatly strengthened their combat ability as a team.

The Chinese table tennis team won unprecedented victories at the 28th world championships in 1965. The players' living study and application of Chairman Mao's works reached a new stage during their pre-championship training. The more they studied the greater their keenness to study, and the more they applied what they studied the better they solved problems. They consciously used Mao Tse-tung's thought to remould their thinking and direct their playing.

Analysing the situation after the 27th world championships, the players drew the conclusion that the men's team should guard against conceit and carry on an uninterrupted revolution in order to defend their winning records. The women's team should draw lessons from the previous championships and redouble their efforts to win victories.

Some of the girls, however, were found to be lacking the necessary will and determination. They were still worried by personal gain or loss in the coming championships. With this problem in mind, they studied Chairman Mao's works.

Members of the men's team also lent a helping hand. A talk given by Hsu Yin-sheng analysed, in a vivid and penetrating way, the problems among the women   players. He stressed that sportsmen must foster a revolutionary world outlook, place the glory of the country above other considerations, train and compete with a strong class feeling and with the "foe" in mind. He also advised the girls to use the method of "one divides into two" to handle problems arising in the course of training and competition. The talk was regarded as a very good summing-up of the experience of the Chinese table tennis team in studying and applying Chairman Mao's works over the years.

On January 12, 1965, Chairman Mao read the text of Hsu Yin-sheng's talk and said it was a good piece of writing, full of dialectical materialism. Chairman Mao's comment helped the masses look at philosophy as something not "mysterious" and opened a new epoch in which the workers, peasants and soldiers grasp philosophy directly.

To the Chinese table tennis team, Chairman Mao's comment has been a tremendous inspiration to advance triumphantly. In the course of preparing for the 28th world championships, they have placed the study and application of Chairman Mao's works in the forefront and put revolutionary dialectics into practice. They said that Mao Tse-tung's thought was a far more important weapon than the table tennis bat and that the bat should be placed under the command of his thought.

Chairman Mao's comment gave members of the

women's team great strength, sharpened their eyes and opened out their thinking. They set out for the world championships with great determination to win. Stepping forward to accept the Corbillon Cup at the 28th world championships, Lin Hui-ching, a stalwart of the Chinese women's team, said to her team-mates: "We owe our victory to the great thought of Mao Tse-tung".

Though winning tremendous glory for the country, members of the Chinese team were not conceited. They used the sharp weapon of Mao Tse-tung's thought to open fire on their own shortcomings and errors. World champion Chuang Tse-tung wrote an article full of the spirit of self-criticism.

When asked why they criticised themselves after winning so many world titles, members of the Chinese team said: "Chairman Mao has told us that we have taken but the very first step in our 10,000-li long march and that it will take great efforts to safeguard what we have won. In order to defend our world titles, we must raise the level of play and this in turn demands that we raise our ideological level". One of them said: "There is a limit to winning world championships but there is no limit to serving the people. We must start from scratch all over again and carry on an uninterrupted revolution".

"Strike at the root and start from scratch"—this is a militant slogan full of the thorough-going revolutionary spirit of the proletariat as well as an important experience of the Chinese table tennis team in using Mao Tse-tung's thought to transform the subjective and objective worlds.

After the 28th world championships, the Chinese players brought their movement to study and apply Chairman's Mao's works to a new height. They take Chairman Mao's works as the supreme guide for all their actions and have made great efforts to apply what they study.

During their recent tours of Japan, Cambodia and Syria, the Chinese players snatched every bit of available time to study Chairman Mao's works, while travelling, in hotels or any other place, even during days of packed programmes of competition. They regarded the study as their primary need and consistently acted in a spirit of thorough-going revolution.

At a recent discussion, the Chinese players agreed that "armed with Mao Tse-tung's thought, we shall have the greatest unity, the clearest sight, the greatest courage and the highest morale. We shall fear neither monsters and demons in the class struggle, nor strong opponents in playing".

NCNA, 26 August 1966

FAITH SAVING

. . . On 5 October last year, a motorized fishing boat with a full catch of prawns received an order from the production headquarters: "Fierce winds tonight; return to harbour for shelter at once". As the boat was homeward bound that night, the wind rose and churned up big waves that swept into the hold. The wind drove the wooden fishing boat onto a shoal, damaging the bottom of the vessel and the rudder. The seas poured into the hold, endangering the lives of the 16 comrades on board.

The crew took this teaching of Chairman Mao's as their highest fighting order: **"This army has an indomitable spirit and is determined to vanquish all enemies and never to yield"**. With great composure, they went into action to fight the storm. At this critical moment, the squadron leader, Chen Chao, a communist, was worried about the safety of the motorized fishing boat behind theirs and turned on the danger signal light to warn it against making further advance.

The engine room was swamping badly, and the boat

might go down at any moment. At this crucial juncture, the chief engineer, Ma Ching-hsi, Wang Shih-chiang, a demobilized soldier, and a communist youth league member, Li Chih-an, jumped into the engine room and helped bail out the water. Seeing a portrait of Chairman Mao on the steering tower, Li Chih-an, at the danger of being swept away by the wind and waves, climbed up and brought the portrait down and held it high in his hands. Seeing this, the comrades were filled with immense strength. As the men bailed, they recited in unison these passages from Chairman Mao's writings: **"Be resolute, fear no sacrifice, and surmount every difficulty to win victory"**, and **"To die for the people is weightier than Mount Tai"**.

Soon the engine was under water and the fishing boat continued sinking. The squadron leader, Chen Chao, experienced in sea battles, reminded himself of this teaching of Chairman Mao's: **"The party organization should be composed of the advanced elements of the proletariat; it should be a vigorous vanguard organization capable of leading the proletariat and the revolutionary masses in the fight against the class enemy"**.

At this critical moment he called an enlarged emergency meeting of the party group to use Mao Tse-tung's thought to unify the thinking and action of all the comrades. The meeting decided to divide the crew into two groups each taking one life raft. Each group would be a fighting unit in line with Chairman Mao's teaching, **"All people in the revolutionary ranks must care for each other, must love and help each other"**.

The members left all their personal belongings behind when they abandoned ship, but took portraits of Chairman Mao, the great leader's writings, and the red-star national flag of their motherland. Just before they left, they stood waist deep in water on the deck, arms linked and, facing toward Peking, they wished our great leader Chairman Mao a long, long life, and recited his instructions and sang revolutionary songs. Then their life-raft made for Tientsin, the nearest port.

They had to strain every muscle to advance in the icy seas in the teeth of the gale and rain, but they drew infinite strength from the portrait of Chairman Mao. They kept the life rafts going and struggled on unflinchingly in the raging waves. They were inspired by these heroic lines from one of Chairman Mao's poems: **"I care not that the wind blows and the waves beat; it is better than idly strolling in a courtyard"**.

The wind grew stronger at dawn. The 16 fishermen, who had fought the wind and waves a whole night, did what they usually do. They faced the portrait of Chairman Mao and wished the great leader a long, long life. Then they sang *The East Is Red*. This was followed by a recitation of Chairman Mao's great teaching: **"In times of difficulty we must not lose sight of our achievements, must see the bright future, and must pluck up our courage"**. Then they sang songs of quotations from Chairman Mao.

While fighting against the waves and gale, the squadron leader caught hold of a bamboo pole which was drifting nearby. He told the chief engineer to take out the national flag and attach it to the pole. Soon, the five-star red flag flew over the territorial waters of the motherland.

When news of the accident reached the leading body of the P.L.A. units in the area, speed boats and aeroplanes were immediately sent out. A dozen government institutions and state enterprises in the Tientsin area also sent out about a 100 boats to search Pohai Bay.

In order to save their class brothers, the fishermen on two fishing boats, each with a capacity of no more than 60 tons, risked their own lives to take part in the rescue operation. They sailed their boats at full speed against the gale. Finally, they spotted the liferafts and saved the fishermen who had been fighting waves and wind for 12 hours. At that moment, the fishermen recalled how in the old society fishermen died at sea whenever there was a storm. Thoughts of their present happiness contrasted with their former sufferings brought tears to the eyes of everyone present. They cheered: "Long live Chairman Mao!" "A long, long life to Chairman Mao!"

Peking Radio, 23 February 1969

BRAVING THE TUNNEL

. . . Difficulties grew as the tunnel bored deeper into the mountains. When it reached a depth of more than 100 metres, the smoke given off by the explosives could not be cleared away easily. Because of this [the men] suffered from headaches and watery eyes. As the tunnel went still deeper, it was difficult even to light matches and explosive fuses due to the lack of oxygen. Many people fainted at work.

Were they to become disheartened and give up, or advance with courage? It was a serious test. Mao Tse-tung thought study classes were run on the construction site. A revolutionary mass criticism campaign was launched, using Mao Tse-tung thought as the weapon to criticize and repudiate thoroughly the "philosophy of survival" advocated by the renegade, hidden traitor and scab Liu Shao-chi. The builders became determined to carry on in the revolutionary spirit of fearing neither hardship nor death and contribute their last ounce of strength to the revolution.

Kuo Hung-yu, leader of a detachment of the builders, had a headache as soon as he entered the tunnel. He summoned up all his strength to wield the heavy hammer. Dense smoke in the tunnel choked him and soon he fell unconscious. He was taken out by his comrades. When he regained consciousness, he silently recited Chairman Mao's teaching: **"What is work? Work is struggle. A good comrade is one who is more eager to go where the difficulties are greater"**, and immediately went back into the tunnel. He fell down unconscious three times that day but did not leave the job . . .

Peking Radio, 11 November 1969

TURNING THE TIDE

. . . The commanders and fighters of a certain unit sped to the scene of disaster from some 700 li away with steamboats, ferryboats and rubber boats. Following the tradition of **"Give full play to our style of fighting: courage in battle, no fear of sacrifice, no fear of fatigue, and continuous fighting (that is, fighting successive battles in a short time without rest)"**, they travelled two days and one night continually, and made four daring attempts to rescue the stranded masses.

In the first attempt, Liu Hsien-chen, a squad leader who is also a Commmunist Party member, fainted upon arrival at the scene after pulling the boats for seven consecutive hours without taking any food for a whole day and night. However, he was not intimidated by either hunger or fatigue. As soon as he regained consciousness, he immediately called a party group meeting. He said: "communist party members must give full play to the revolutionary spirit of fearing neither hardship nor death. We must surmount all difficulties, and fulfill our task".

Chin Yuan-ching, a new fighter, said: "We are armed with Mao Tse-tung thought, and Communist Party members have given us a good example. We must save the poor and lower-middle peasants even at the cost of our lives!"

Chin could not swim and was small in stature. While helping the other comrades in arms push the boat into the water, he was suddenly caught in a strong current. He shouted "Long live Chairman Mao!" before he was swallowed by the waves. The comrades in arms pulled him up. While he was still unconscious he shouted: "Squad leader. . . let me go down. . . I have not fulfilled my task!"

The civilian workers stranded at the irrigation worksite on the Ta River in Shoukuang County also carried out a fierce battle against the tidal wave. Over 170 workers of the No. 5 company of Wangkao commune were surrounded by water on a small mound only six metres in diameter. With the water rapidly rising, this elevated spot was soon to be submerged. However, they were not at all afraid. Holding high a picture of Chairman Mao and a book of Chairman Mao's quotations, they read his instructions again and again. Wang Hanmin, political instructor of the workers, said to them: "In battling with the waves, we must act as though we were battling with our enemies. As long as we are all united against the enemy, any difficulty can be overcome". Under his leadership, everyone forgot their fatigue. They used their bedding and mats, together with mud, as a dam to check the rising water. Seven times the rising water was checked this way, with the dam being raised each time. The wind and rain were becoming stronger and stronger, and wave after wave lashed their small mound. Suddenly, their dam was breached and the rushing water threatened to submerge the mound. The workers quickly used their own bodies as a human wall to fill in the breach, while others, with only a few hoes or their own hands, dug more earth to raise the dam and fill the gap. This victory was finally achieved after three hours of hard battle.

Chairman Mao has taught us: **"Difficulty is never an unconquerable monster. If everyone takes part in the battle, it will be overcome"**. The tidal wave finally had to submit to the united fighting power of the masses . . .

Peking Radio, 28 May 1969

SPIRITUAL ATOM-BOMB AIDS HARVEST

. . . In 1968 the Tachai brigade experienced a severe drought and hailstorm. Hailstones as big as eggs fell on the cornfields, piling up two to three inches. Corn stems were broken and rice seedlings crushed; part of the crop was uprooted. Potatoes and beans were smashed completely. But no matter how destructive the hailstorm, it did not destroy the poor and lower-middle peasants who were armed with Mao Tse-tung's thought. They said confidently: "We run into natural calamities every year and we fight them one by one. We are sure of our victory over natural calamities this year!

"We used our hands to save the battered corn and rice. Man and woman, young and old, we worked day and night and everyone did the work of two men. Our efforts proved that a bad thing can lead to good results after all. Through our struggles we turned a calamity-stricken year into one of bumper harvests."

The poor and lower-middle peasants said with animation: "Bumper harvests do not come from heaven or from earth. They come from Mao Tse-tung's thought'. **'Natural calamities are like paper tigers. If you are afraid of them, they will conquer you; if you fight them, you will find them not so powerful'.** Equipped with Mao Tse-tung's thought, our strength is inexhaustible and we can be most resourceful. Even though we work day in and day out, we do not feel tired or complain in times of hardship. It is through these disasters that our cadres and the broad masses, particularly the younger generation, were tested and educated.

"Chairman Mao has taught us: **'We advocate self-reliance"**. With the spirit of hard struggle, we, the poor and lower-middle peasants, displayed the heroism of **'Dare to make the sun and moon shine in new skies.'** " Thus flooded lands were turned into fertile fields, barren mountains became forests, river water was pumped to the highlands, and grain production greatly increased. Commune members had new housing and the old Tachai became a new socialist production brigade.

Comrade Lin Piao said: "Once Mao Tse-tung's thought is grasped by the broad masses, it becomes an inexhaustible source of strength and a spiritual atom bomb of infinite power". The Tachai peasants have attached first importance to the movement of creative study and application of Mao Tse-tung's thought. That is why we have revolutionized our thinking and acquired the correct idea of working the land for the sake of the revolution and in the interests of the people . . .

Peking Radio, 2 January 1969

CANCER IS A PAPER TIGER

. . . In September 1968, Wang Te-ming went to hospital for a check up. The cancer had spread to the lungs, and it appeared to be a late stage of cancer.

Confronted with life or death, Wang Te-ming thought of the victories won during the great proletarian cultural revolution, and took his mind off the serious state of his health. Revolutionary committees had been set up in all the provinces and autonomous regions (except Taiwan Province) of China by September 1968. This inspired Wang Te-ming and he recalled the happy moment when he saw our great leader Chairman Mao during the second air force conference of activists in the living study and application of Chairman Mao's works, which he had attended. This gave him inexhaustible strength. On that very day, he conscientiously studied Chairman Mao's teachings: **"Imperialism and all reactionaries are paper tigers"** and **"This army has an indomitable spirit and is determined to vanquish all enemies and never to yield"**. He thought to himself: "Like imperialism and all reactionaries, cancer is nothing but a

paper tiger. One must take cancer as an enemy, and
never yield or surrender to it, but use invincible Mao
Tse-tung thought to conquer it".

Inspired by Mao Tse-tung thought and under the
careful treatment of the revolutionary medical workers,
Wang Te-ming finally conquered the cancer . . .

NCNA, 14 September 1969

OPERATING WITH SEWING NEEDLES

. . . The operation presented considerable difficulties because the clinic lacked proper equipment and Li Hsun-
chao had never performed such a complicated operaton
before. In line with Chairman Mao's teachings, he boldly
overcame the difficulties. He used ordinary sewiing
needles as operating needles, made pincers do as forceps
and used razor blades instead of scalpels. Under the
guidance of the invincible Mao Tse-tung thought, he
completed the operation successfully. After one and a
half months' meticulous treatment, he finally cured the
sore on Lo Huai-wang's back. Lo Huai-wang said with
deep emotion: "It is Chairman Mao's revolutionary line
which saved my life. I will always be loyal to Chairman
Mao and never falter though the seas run dry and the
mountains crumble!"

It was just at that time that the capitalist roaders in
the county health department sent people to check up on
Li Hsun-chao's work. They said that since Li Hsun-chao
was not a surgeon he had no business operating on
patients as he thought fit and that he had violated the
system of medical treatment. Li Hsun-chao replied:
"Chairman Mao teaches us to serve the people whole-
heartedly. To relieve our class brothers' suffering, I
dared to climb a mountain of swords and cross a sea of

fire". Guided by Chairman Mao's line for medical and health work and supported by the poor and lower-middle peasants, he continued to give medical treatment to his patients and performed more than 300 operations.

Peking Radio, 8 July 1969

OBSERVATION OF SOLAR ECLIPSE DEFEATS IMPERIALISM

China has a long history in observing solar eclipses. More than 3,200 years ago, China's labouring people carried out and recorded the first observation in human history of a total solar eclipse, leaving behind extremely valuable scientific assets.

For a long period in the past, imperialist and modern revisionist countries and a number of bourgeois reactionary academic "authorities" in China monopolized solar eclipse observations and the information obtained. This time, under the guidance of Chairman Mao's proletarian line in scientific research, Chinese workers, poor and lower-middle peasants, People's Liberation Army men, and revolutionary young people and scientists made large-scale and independent comprehensive observations of the total solar eclipse in Sinkiang in the western part of the country and achieved a tremendous success. They have ended the monopoly in modern solar eclipse observation by imperialist and modern revisionist countries and planted the great red banner of Mao Tse-tung's thought in the field of solar eclipse research . . .

. . . The revolutionary scientists and young people were re-educated by workers, peasants and soldiers in the course of the observation project. Armed with the invincible thought of Mao Tse-tung they advanced courageously in scaling world peaks of science and made new contributions.

The airborne observation team arrived at the airport in mid-August, 1968. The members of the team were in high spirits and eager to fly at high altitude to perform their task. In trial-flights, when the plane went above 8,000 metres, some of them vomited, some had acute headaches, some suffered stomach discomfort, and some felt their limbs go numb. When the plane reached an altitude of 10,000 metres some of them had to lie down. Acute high-altitude sickness was a stern test for each member of the team and each fought a fierce ideological struggle in his mind over whether he could face up to the difficulties with courage or wanted to beat a retreat.

At this juncture, P.L.A. comrades led the members of the team in studying Chairman Mao's three constantly articles: *Serve the People*, *In Memory of Norman Bethune* and *The Foolish Old Man Who Removed the Mountains*.

. . . Inspired by Mao Tse-tung's thought, the members of the airborne observation team displayed revolutionary heroism and flew at an altitude of 11,000 metres in a non-hermetically sealed plane cabin, thus breaking the world record set by some foreign countries of airborne observations from a non-hermetically sealed plane cabin at an altitude of 9,000 metres. They therefore achieved the world's most complete airborne observation of a solar eclipse.

NCNA, 23 January 1969

FISHING FOR THE REVOLUTION

Revolutionary fishermen along the coast of Chekiang Province, East China, have made big catches during the current summer fishing season.

They put revolution in command of fishing and set up thousands of Mao Tse-tung thought study classes on their fishing vessels, where they conscientiously studied the documents of the Party Congress. At sea or in harbour, they carried out revolutionary mass criticism and roundly repudiated the revisionist fallacies peddled by the renegade, hidden traitor and scab Liu Shao-chi, such as "material incentives", "skills first" and "profits in command". Bringing into play the revolutionary spirit of hard struggle, the fishermen overcame a number of difficulties, including the low temperature of the water . . .

NCNA, 11 June 1969

WIPING OUT SNAILS

The poor and lower-middle peasants and revolutionary cadres of Liuchuang commune in Nanhui County, their revolutionary spirit of courage and perseverance enhanced by the triumphant opening of the Party's Ninth National Congress, have successfully fulfilled the task of digging up the soil to eliminate snails two days ahead of schedule in spite of rains. These poor and lower-middle peasants and revolutionary cadres have adhered to Chairman Mao's brilliant instruction on the need to wipe out schistosomiasis.

Many old peasants said excitedly: "Chairman Mao is so concerned about the health of us poor and lower-middle peasants! We must follow his teaching to wipe out the snails resolutely and completely" . . .

Shanghai Radio, 8 April 1969

Chapter III

Abnegation of Self

NIGHT-SOIL COLLECTORS

Old poor peasant Yin Yu-tsai suffered bitterly in the old society and hates it with all his heart. But for a period he neglected collective matters because of the poisonous influence of the counter-revolutionary revisionist line of . . . Liu Shao-chi. When his wife and daughter discovered this, they ran a Mao Tse-tung thought study class at home . . . Mao Tse-tung thought has brought great changes to the family. When the brigade's rape fields lacked manure, the family turned out at night when nobody could see them and carried their own night-soil and other manure to the collective fields . . .

Peking Radio, 4 April 1970

SURRENDERING MANURE INSPIRES POEM

. . . "One day, when I went to work in the fields, I saw the plants in one of the team's plots turning yellow. My first thought was to fetch the manure we had at home and put it on this plot. But on second thoughts, I remembered that no fertilizer whatever had as yet been spread on my family's own household plot. What should I do? I turned to Chairman Mao's works for the answer. Chairman Mao says in *In Memory of Norman Bethune:* **'We must all learn the spirit of absolute selfless-**

ness from him. With this spirit everyone can be very useful to the people'. I decided then that all the manure at home ought to be taken to the team's plot.

"After work, when I told my young sister-in-law about this, she said: 'Of course it's a good thing to give the team's land more fertilizer; the only trouble is: what shall we put on our land?' I replied: 'We must not be of two minds about anything that concerns the collective. Giving the fertilizer to the team means increasing production and aiding our country's construction'. Then the two of us studied this teaching of Chairman Mao's: **'At no time and in no circumstances should a Communist place his personal interests first; he should subordinate them to the interests of the nation and of the masses'.** My sister-in-law quickly saw things in the right spirit. At meal-time, we asked the elders what they thought about this and they too agreed with us. That night we sent all the manure at home, 12 cart-loads, to the team's plot. And we all got together to compose this poem:

> *If for a single day we fail to study the works of Chairman Mao,*
> *Selfish thoughts will raise their heads.*

> *By studying Chairman Mao's works every day,*
> *Public interest will take firm root, and self-interest will make way.*

> *Studying Chairman Mao's works together, our family will quickly go forward,*
> *On the broad road of ideological revolutionization.*

> *On the broad road of ideological revolutionization...*

Peking Review, No. 40, 4 October 1968

PURGING SELF WITH CASTOR BEANS

. . . After her family meeting one evening to fight self and repudiate revisionism, Wang Feng-chin, an elderly poor peasant woman, remained sleepless while others were sound asleep. When planting castor beans on land at the edge of the fields, the old woman took a patch of the collective land to plant 14 extra clusters. Her eldest son noticed this. That very evening with his mother he studied Chairman Mao's works and criticized and repudiated the renegade, traitor and scab Liu Shao-chi's theory of "merging private and public interests" at the family meeting to fight self and repudiate revisionism. Chairman Mao's teachings stirred up a sharp ideological struggle in the elderly woman.

The more she thought over this, the greater she felt her selfishness. It was already midnight, but she woke up her daughter-in-law and asked uneasily: "Do you think it was a big mistake for me to plant the extra clusters of castor beans?" Knowing that her mother-in-law was consciously fighting self, she answered: "Yes, mamma, you're on the right track. If you want to know whether you have done right or wrong, you must judge it in the light of Chairman Mao's teaching, or you must judge whether it corresponds to Chairman Mao's revolutionary line, or to Liu Shao-chi's counter-revolutionary revisionist line".

The elderly peasant, thinking over her daughter-in-law's remark, reviewed Chairman Mao's instruction on **"utter devotion to others without any thought of self"**, and she felt she must get rid of the "self" in her mind as soon as possible. So she woke up the whole family, and made self-criticism before them all. She said: "Chairman Mao has urged us time and again to be selfless. These 14 clusters of castor beans I planted on the edge of the brigade's fields do not take up much space, but what I did shows how selfish I am!" She stopped for a moment, and went on: "I was caught in the trap of Liu Shao-chi's theory of "merging private and public interests". One-tenth of an inch taken from the

51

collective land is one inch along Liu Shao-chi's bad line. This time I have to dig out everything that remains of Liu Shao-chi's wicked line from my mind. Only if I do this can I follow Chairman Mao's revolutionary line to communism".

The next day, Wang Feng-chin dug up all the castor beans planted on collective land. She said: "This time I'm not only digging out the castor beans from the ridges, but uprooting self-interest in my mind" . . .

NCNA, 30 March 1969

BAREFOOT DOCTOR'S SACRIFICE

Hsianglan is a "barefoot doctor" of Lisu nationality. Her child had pneumonia. It was running a high fever and, as there was no medicine for the disease in her medical kit, she decided to go and get some from the commune clinic and leave her husband to look after the child. She was so worried about her child that she ran nearly all the way from her village to the clinic and back, a distance of several dozen kilometres. Without stopping to regain her breath, she took up the child, who was already in a coma, to give it an injection. At that moment hurried footsteps were heard, and poor peasant commune member Puaho burst in, carrying a child in her arms. Her child, too, was seriously ill with pneumonia.

Hsianglan had only brought back the medicine for her child. This put her in a quandary. Which child should she treat first?

Chairman Mao's teaching: **"Comrade Bethune's spirit, his utter devotion to others without any thought of self, was shown in his boundless sense of responsibility in his work and his boundless warm-heartedness towards all comrades and the**

people" flashed into her mind. This made it clear what she should do. She told her husband that she thought Puaho's child should have the medicine. Her husband answered: "We should act in the way Chairman Mao teaches us". Without hesitation, Hsianglan gave the other child the injection. When Puaho learnt that the medicine had been meant for Hsianglan's sick child, she could not control her tears of gratitude. "How can I thank you?" Hsianglan and her husband answered in one voice: "Give your thanks to Chairman Mao! It is Chairman Mao who teaches us what to do" .

Peking Radio, 16 June 1969

"HOW CAN WE BE FROSTBITTEN?"

. . . As night fell, the two girls drove the flock into a gully for shelter. They sat on a big stone to rest, but soon they were shivering with cold. The sheep were also cold and would not lie still, some even tried to rush out. The two girls recited aloud Chairman Mao's words, **"Give full play to our style of fighting: courage in battle, no fear of sacrifice, no fear of fatigue, and continuous fighting (that is, fighting successive battles in a short time without rest)".** They got up and ran around the flock. In this way they calmed the sheep and warmed themselves up. They said delightedly: "Let us run, this will not only protect the flock, but also keep us warm. As long as we are alive, we must see that they are safe". They ran around and around the flock with hardly a pause all night.

As dawn broke, the snowstorm died out. The red sun rose in the east. Shu-ying and Tieh-mei could not help singing the revolutionary song, *A Long, Long Life to Chairman Mao.*

The commune revolutionary committee and the fronier guard unit sent many comrades out to look for Shu-ying and Tieh-mei. The sound of singing drew the searchers' attention and they soon found the two girls. They asked in concern: "Are you frostbitten?" The two girls who had come from the city answered with a smile: "With the bright sun shining down on us, how can we be frostbitten!"

So Shu-ying and Tieh-mei were safe and sound, along with the collective's 356 sheep. Facing the rising sun, all those present cheered: "Long live Chairman Mao, a long long life to him!" . . .

Peking Radio, 2 March 1969

STRICKEN PEASANTS REFUSE RELIEF

. . . Most of those who regularly studied Chairman Mao's works before were cadres, young and middle-aged peasants and others who know how to read. Now with the establishment of the family study classes, everyone is studying. They use Chairman Mao's brilliant three constantly read articles as their weapon to criticize Liu Shao-chi's theory of "merging public and private interest" and turn their families into battlefronts where they fight self-interest and encourage devotion to the public interest.

The area was hit by a drought last summer which menaced 86 hectares of rice fields in the brigade. The state sent pumps and diesel engines to the area. Should the brigade accept state aid? This topic was discussed by the poor and lower-middle peasants at their family study classes. They all said they would meet the challenge of drought in the spirit of self reliance, so that the government could send the machines and diesel oil to areas where they were more needed. The peasants set to work and used waterwheels and other devices to irrigate the land and defeat the drought.

Following this a tornado destroyed more than 100 rooms in the brigade. The state appropriated relief funds. The poor and lower-middle peasants again studied at their family classes Chairman Mao's teachings on self-reliance. They decided not to accept a penny from the state. Relying on the invincible thought of Mao Tse-tung, they overcame the difficulties caused by the natural disasters. Returns after the autumn harvest showed that in 1968 the brigade harvested 50 tons more grain than in the preceding year. The poor and lower-middle peasants decided to sell more surplus grain to the state . . .

Peking Radio, 14 April 1969

RELUCTANT WIVES FALL IN LINE

. . . In the beginning the wives of a few cadres harboured the idea of "It is not worthwhile to be a cadre", because their husbands, after becoming cadres, were so busy with work that they had no time to pay attention to their families. They felt they could still have a good life working for their living, without having to become cadres.

Focusing on these erroneous concepts, the production brigade revolutionary committee gave the wives class education in the study classes. After this education, many of the wives spoke with all sincerity that holding back the cadres means, in fact, holding back the dictatorship of the proletariat. There can be no good life if we lose our political power and the country changes colour.

Chang Cheng-kun, of Changchia production team, after becoming the leader of the revolutionary leading group, was kept all day long in the hills by his wife, who would not let him become a cadre. Later, his wife entered the study class, and her awareness was enhanced. She then not only did not attempt to hold him back any longer, but attempted to lead by example in speech and action.

In the fight against the July waterlogging, this couple was in the fields day and night. The grandmother wanted the wife to stay at home and take care of the children, but the wife said that the battle against waterlogging could be won only when cadres' dependents were in the front-lines. She even mobilized her grandmother to join in the struggle. Very quickly a deeply moving scene emerged in the production team—showing men and women, young and old, taking to the frontlines en masse to work with one mind to stem the floodwaters.

After the revolutionary zeal of the cadres' wives had been aroused, the revolutionary committeee of the pro-duction brigade further stimulated this zeal by applying the method of grasping typical examples and holding discussion-application meetings. Liu Tsuan-i, wife of Li Kuang-fu, leading member of Tsaichia production team's leading group and concurrently member of the produc-tion brigade revolutionary committee, put public interest to the fore, creatively studied Mao Tse-tung thought, and became a great help to her husband, a leader of the masses.

Nanking, Kiangsu Provincial Broadcast, 24 November 1969

"CHILDREN ARE PRECIOUS WEALTH OF THE PARTY AND PEOPLE"

. . . "I have three children, the eldest is 10 years old and the youngest is only four. I used to pamper the children. I only knew how to love them by attending to their mate-rial needs and did not know how to look after them ideologically and politically. Starting from my own interests, I let my children go to school at an early age, hoping they would go through middle school and university education, learn a profession and get good jobs. I thought this would bring me fame and when I'm old they would support me. I never thought of educating the children with a view to consolidating the dictatorship of the proletariat.

"Chairman Mao teaches us: **'In order to guarantee that our Party and country do not change their colour, we must not only have a correct line and correct policies but must train and bring up millions of successors who will carry on the cause of proletarian revolution'**. The emergence of re-visionism in the Soviet Union has given me a painful lesson. When I pondered over this and the way I used to educate my children, I was greatly shocked. Paying attention only to the children's food and clothing while neglecting their ideological and political upbringing, as I did, would make the children grow up as the offspring of revisionism, and they would never become successors to the revolutionary cause of the proletariat. If we bring up the young generation in this way, there is the danger that some day we would lose political power. It makes me feel uneasy when I think of this.

"In the old society I never had enough to eat and wear. Carrying along a basket, I went begging here and there every day. At night I found shelter under the eaves. When it grew cold, I huddled myself in dry straw. Dear are our parents, but dearer still is Chairman Mao to us; deep are rivers and seas, but deeper still is the goodness of Chairman Mao. We owe what we are to Chairman Mao. We suffered in the old society because political power was not in our hands. Therefore, political power is the lifeline of us poor people. Being future successors to revolution, children are precious wealth of the Party and people.

"Chairman Mao points out: **'Basing themselves on the changes in the Soviet Union, the imperialist**

prophets are pinning their hopes of "peaceful evolution" on the third or fourth generation of the Chinese Party. We must shatter these imperialist prophecies'. Chairman Mao's teaching raises the important question of whether the proletarian revolutionary cause will have its successors and of how to prevent the tragedy in the Soviet Union from being repeated in China. To pay attention to the political and ideological education of the children means to bring up and educate them with Mao Tse-tung thought so that they will always be loyal to Chairman Mao, to Mao Tse-tung thought and to Chairman Mao's revolutionary line, thus ensuring that our Party will not turn revisionist nor will our state change its political colour. This is the biggest responsibility of us parents.

"In the course of educating children, I have come to understand that when we bring up the children according to self-interest, we are training them in the interest of the bourgeoisie. When we nurture them with Mao Tse-tung thought, we are training them in the interests of the people and state.

"My children have grown up under the Red flag and in happiness. They do not know the sufferings in the old society and therefore do not appreciate the happiness in the new society as much as they should.

"Chairman Mao teaches us: **'Never forget class struggle'**. To forget class struggle is to forget political power. I think the most essential thing in educating children is to arm their minds with the concept of class struggle and to enable them to distinguish between ourselves and the enemy and between right and wrong from childhood. With the children's living ideas in my mind I often lead them to visit the class education exhibitions. I tell the children stories which I myself compose to describe the crimes of the landlords and capitalists in oppressing and exploiting the poor people in the old society.

"I tell the children the sufferings of the poor people in the old society because they held no political power, and contrast this to their happiness in the new society when they hold political power. I also recount the hardships which Chairman Mao went through in leading the revolutionary people to seize political power, and describe Chairman Mao's wisdom and greatness. Having understood the source of the past sufferings and today's happiness, the children become not so particular over food and clothing as before. Instead they study Chairman Mao's writings with class feelings.

"In giving education in the struggle between Chairman Mao's proletarian revolutionary line and Liu Shao-chi's counter-revolutionary revisionist line, I took Liu Shao-chi and the handful of party persons in power taking the capitalist road as teachers by negative examples. I repeatedly told my children of the towering crimes committed by the capitalist roaders in opposing the Party, opposing socialism and opposing Mao Tse-tung thought that were exposed in the great cultural revolution. I took them to read the big-character posters.

"On the streets I often sat together with them to criticize Liu Shao-chi's reactionary trash of 'exploitation has its merits', 'san tzu i pao' (the extension of plots for private use, the extension of free markets, the increase in the number of small enterprises with sole responsibility for their own profits or losses, and the fixing of output quotas on the basis of individual households), and 'four freedoms' (freedom to practice usury, to hire labour, to buy or sell land and to engage in private enterprise). I held meetings to criticise and denounce the renegade hidden traitor and scab Liu Shao-chi at my courtyard in my spare time, each of which was usually attended by a dozen children. I also help them organize a theatrical team, and rehearse short items in praise of Chairman Mao's revolutionary line and repudiating the arch renegade Liu Shao-chi. They present these items in the streets, at railway stations and in production teams.

"Under continuous education, the children have a bitter hatred for Liu Shao-chi and have a profound love for Chairman Mao. They do not think first of their father or mother, brother or sister, but think of our great leader

Chairman Mao.

"In the current earth-shaking cultural revolution I have learned the following truth: under the powerful dictatorship of the proletariat, when the class enemy tries to overthrow our political power, he often takes advantage of the thought of 'self' in our mind. In educating the children, we should have a clear cut stand and help the children to distinguish between the bourgeois ideas and the proletarian ideas. We should make them not only hate revisionism but hate the thought of 'self' in their own minds. Having Mao Tse-tung thought in their minds from childhood, they will be able to tell what is right and what is wrong and fight self and criticize revisionism.

"In order to help the children distinguish the bourgeois ideas from the proletarian ideas, I tell them about the three brilliant images in the three constantly read articles by Chairman Mao, as well as the feats of heroes and models who gave everything for the public interest. I point out to them in daily life what is a bourgeois idea and what is a proletarian idea. Once little Li went to school with shabby clothes on. When she came home in the evening she said: 'Mama, my clothes are ugly, would you make new ones for me?' Starting from her word 'ugly', I told her about Chairman Mao's teachings on hard work and plain living. I said: 'One with bourgeois ideas looks upon worn-out clothes as ugly, but one with proletarian ideas disapproves of the bourgeois habit of decking oneself up and thinks that ugly'. Little Li said: 'I now know that it is the bourgeois ideas that make one see the worn-out clothes as ugly'. She wore the same clothes to school the next day, happily.

I often help my children to reveal and criticize their selfish thoughts. This quickly raises their ability to distinguish the good from the bad in the light of Mao Tse-tung thought and their consciousness of fighting self. One day I returned from the fields. Before I went into the house, little Li ran to me and said: 'Mama, some children are fighting. I asked them to stop fighting. I tried to persuade them for a long time, but they wouldn't listen. You'd better go quickly and help them solve their contradictions!' I replied, 'I have no time to bother about the children's affairs!' Before I finished my words, little Li criticized me. She said: 'Chairman Mao teaches us: **"Our duty is to hold ourselves responsible to the people. Every word, every act and every policy must conform to the people's interests."** You are the chairman of the neighbourhood committee. It is selfishness not wanting to bother about the children's fighting. That means you are not acting according to Chairman Mao's instructions and not holding yourself responsible for your work to the people'. The girl's criticism made me blush. But from her criticism I saw the growth of the new generation and this made me very happy".

NCNA, 1 June 1969

MODEL FAMILY

... "Not long after I got married, my husband joined the P.L.A. I lived with his parents. At first they treated me like their own daughter. When singing activities were organized in the production team and I was asked to join to learn songs like *The Poor and Lower-Middle Peasants Are of One Heart*, Mother-in-law told me: 'Go, Yueh-hsiang. If we poor and lower-middle peasants don't sing these songs, who should?' When the masses elected me to be a cadre, Father-in-law said: 'Take the job, Yueh-hsiang. If we poor and lower-middle peasants don't become cadres, who should?' But after I became a cadre in the production brigade, a new problem cropped up, that is, I had less and less time for housework. As time went by, Mother-in-law grew a bit annoyed.

"One day, at a family meeting to study Chairman Mao's *Serve the People*, we were discussing how to devote ourselves wholeheartedly to serving the people and to work entirely in their interests. Mother-in-law made a self-criticism. She said: 'Yueh-hsiang, you're busy all day long working in the fields or attending meetings. Father, too, has his hands full looking after the draught animals for the production team. So it's only natural that I should do more of the housework—that's serving the people too. But lately my self-interest has got the better of me: I've been getting annoyed—it's the way you both walk out as soon as you finish a meal and leave me all the work at home. I even thought sometimes that we might as well live apart and each cook his own meals; that I'd wash my hands of the whole thing. But after these few days of study, I've begun to see things differently. My thoughts are certainly a long way from Mao Tse-tung's thought. From now on, I'll try to be like you and put public interest first'.

"This self-criticism touched me to the heart and my words tumbled out: 'Mother, I really have been doing too little housework. I knew you were annoyed, but I thought: Since we've been living together, I've been working in the daytime and going to meetings or doing propaganda work at night. I get all tired out, but when I come back I have to face your unhappy looks. Sometimes, I thought: We might as well call it quits. If things go on like this, our relations are only going to get worse. Of course, this way of thinking was wrong. Chairman Mao teaches us to learn from Comrade Bethune's spirit of **"utter devotion to others without any thoughts of self"**. But I didn't do that. On the contrary, I thought of myself first before thinking of others. From now on, I'll try not only to be a good cadre but also to help you as much as I can with the housework'.

"After fighting self in this heart-to-heart exchange of thoughts, Mother-in-law and I felt much closer to each other. My younger sister-in-law then began to air her thoughts. 'You each had your faults, so have I. I'm not a child any more, but I act like one and stay idle whenever I've free time. I should help Mother do some work, but I've not been very eager. That shows that I lack enthusiasm in working for the revolution. Chairman Mao says that **"all people in the revolutionary ranks must care for each other, must love and help each other"**. From now on, I will pay more heed to Chairman Mao's teachings and do more for the collective'.

"Then my younger brother-in-law also volunteered to play less and help his mother more. He promised to cut fodder for the team's draught animals every day after school.

"The last to speak up was Father-in-law. He said: 'When your mother-in-law was out of temper these last few days, I got irritated too. What I thought was: Taking care of these draught animals is no easy job; you're busy all day long and you don't get results without a lot of effort. If I spend too much time on the job, then work at home is sure to suffer. . . . Then I thought: This way of thinking is all wrong. It is obviously selfish. If I don't curb it but let it grow, it'll become terrible! If it concerns the collective, the smallest matter is important; if it concerns one's self, the biggest matter is unimportant. From now on we must measure all our thoughts with the yardstick of working "entirely" and "wholeheartedly" for the people. We must follow Chairman Mao's instructions. Whatever he says, we'll do.'

"This is an instance of how my family regularly airs thoughts of self-interest and fights against them. Sometimes such revelations and criticisms make one blush with shame. I think this is what is called touching one's soul. Only so can the fight against self-interest be effective. Because we have acted in this way, the relations between members of our family are fine . . .

Wei Yueh-hsiang

Peking Review, No. 40, 4 October 1968

CUTTING HAIR FOR THE REVOLUTION

A barber's shop in Liaoyuan, Kirin Province, North-east China, is described by workers, peasants and soldiers as close to their hearts. Changes in this barber's shop show the transformation in China's service trades as a result of tempering in the great proletarian cultural revolution launched more than two years ago.

The Tungfeng barber's shop is an advanced collective in this city in the live study and application of Mao Tsetung's thought to guide their thinking and actions. It serves workers, peasants and soldiers whole-heartedly. Its service is known for tens of kilometres around.

In adhering to serving workers, peasants and soldiers, the barber's shop has gone through a strenuous struggle between the proletarian revolutionary line and the bourgeois reactionary line.

Set up by workers and peasants in 1958, the barber's shop has followed this road from the beginning. It was welcomed by the masses. But the handful of capitalist-roaders later tried to make the barber's shop stop serving these people by peddling "profits first", "material incentives" and other revisionist nonsense of the arch scab Liu Shao-chi. The capitalist-roaders made the shop serve the bourgeois overlords and ladies by adding costly haircutting equipment and going in for weird hair-dos. They compelled the shop to adopt a piece-work system in their efforts to corrupt the thinking of the barbers.

The workers and peasants and the revolutionary barbers fought against this. They said: "This is our barber's shop, we will not allow anyone to lead it astray". Supported by the revolutionary masses, the barbers of this shop refused to give weird hair-dos such as the capitalist-roaders wanted. They went to the factories, construction sites, workers' residential districts and the outskirts to give haircuts to the workers and peasants.

In the great proletarian cultural revolution, Mao Tse-tung thought has been unprecedentedly popularized and spread on a wide scale. This barber's shop launched a new upsurge in the live study and application of Mao Tse-tung thought. The barbers earnestly study Chairman Mao's works, especially the three constantly read articles. Every one of them takes this teaching, **"utter devotion to others without any thought of self"**, as his constant reminder and serves the people whole-heartedly.

Their hours of service are not fixed. Whenever the workers, peasants and soldiers need a haircut they will serve them. For the convenience of the masses, they send barbers to give haircuts in the factories, villages and neighbourhood communities. They are very familiar with the needs of the people in the area. For instance, these barbers know what work they do, how many members there are in the family, and how often they need haircuts. They also go to the homes of people who are aged, weak, sick or crippled to give them haircuts. These barbers help to fetch water, cut firewood, or wash bedding for them. Some workers and peasants are so occupied with grasping revolution and promoting production that they have no time to come to the shop to get a haircut. The barbers go to their homes after work. Sometimes they find the customers are not at home, and the barber will make a second or third call.

One evening a barber named Chih Sung-ta went out as usual to a residential district to give people haircuts while publicizing the excellent situation of the great proletarian cultural revolution. He returned home late at night. He stayed awake and tossed in his bed as he assessed his day's work in the light of Chairman Mao's teachings. Chih Sung-ta felt uneasy because, when he was cutting the hair of a paralysed man, he noticed that his blanket was soiled and he had not washed it for the sick man. He had failed to work wholly and "entirely" in the people's interests, as taught by Chairman Mao. Early the next morning he went to the home of the man and took the blanket to wash it for him.

The spare-time Mao Tse-tung thought propaganda team set up by the barbers goes from house to house to disseminate the latest instructions of Chairman Mao the moment they are published. Whenever barber Li Shou-wu goes out on an errand or to a meeting, he takes along his hair-clippers and other tools as well as musical instruments. He publicizes Mao Tse-tung thought when travelling in cars or trains, and whenever he has the opportunity, he gives passengers free haircuts.

When this instruction of Chairman Mao's, **"It is highly necessary for young people with education to go to the countryside to be re-educated by the poor and lower-middle peasants"**, was published, the barbers studied it that very night and then went out to publicize it in the neighbourhood communities. Because of the efforts of the barbers, many city dwellers and young people with education happily made the choice to go and settle down in the rural areas.

Peking Radio, 22 April 1969

Chapter IV
Class Love

CLASS LOVE OVERRIDES WIFE'S DEATH

At about 11 o'clock in the morning of December 15 last year, Tso Chia-fa was at a meeting when a comrade ran in shouting: "Old Tso! Your wife has been knocked down by a lorry!"

This was a bolt out of the blue. He rushed to the casualty ward. The political commissar of the hospital was there with the doctors who were already working to save Tso's wife.

What should he do in the face of this disaster? He recalled Chairman Mao's teaching: **"Our point of departure is . . . to proceed in all cases from the interests of the people and not from one's self-interest or from the interests of a small group . . ."** Yes, thought Tso, no matter how great is the misfortune one may meet, it is a small thing when compared to our revolutionary cause—and in dealing with this disaster, I must not start from self-interest, but from the interests of the people.

An anxious crowd had gathered outside the emergency ward, waiting—leaders of the revolutionary mass organizations of the lorry team involved in the accident and responsible comrades of the lorry depot, the transport company and the communications and transport bureau.

Tso Chia-fa was very moved by the concern shown by these proletarian revolutionary comrades. They had many heavy responsibilities at this stage of the great proletarian cultural revolution. Yet, here they were, so worried about his wife and himself. He felt uneasy in his mind.

When they grasped his hands and said "We're terribly sorry for . . . " he interrupted them. "Thank you all", he said. "I promise you that I'll never let this mar the relations like those of fish to water that exist between the army and the people. Let us all act as Chairman Mao teaches us." He opened his *Quotations From Chairman Mao Tse-tung* and together they read the passage: **"We hail from all corners of the country and have joined together for a common revolutionary objective"**. These words made Tso Chia-fa and all the other comrades feel very close.

Then a nurse came out. "Comrade Cheng Yu-chih (Tso's wife) is. . . . " She could not finish the sentence.

Tso Chia-fa and Cheng Yu-chih were comrades very close to each other and had been married for nearly 10 years. Her death was a great shock to him but at this moment of grief Tso Chia-fa recalled Chairman Mao's great teaching: **"A communist should . . . be more concerned about the Party and the masses than about any individual, and more concerned about others than about himself."** He thought of Norman Bethune, whose utter devotion to others without any thought of self had always been a source of inspiration to him. He remembered the last words of the heroic platoon leader Li Wen-chung:"Don'tworry about me. Save the Red Guards!" As these thoughts flashed through his mind, Tso Chia-fa felt full of new strength. "Don't feel sorry for me", he said. "Our most important task at the moment is to devote all our energy to following closely Chairman Mao's great strategic plan and carrying the great proletarian cultural revolution through to the end. No matter what happens we must always be loyal to Chairman Mao, we must be thoroughgoing proletarian revolutionaries".

He added: "What's happened has happened, and nothing can alter it. Don't blame the driver too much.

He must be very upset, and so must those comrades over at the depot. I'll go and see them soon".

He took out of his pocket some shining badges with the portrait of Chairman Mao and pinned one on each comrade's chest.

All were moved to tears by this veteran revolutionary fighter armed by Mao Tse-tung's thought, who was utterly devoted to others without any thought of self. With tears in their eyes, they all shouted: "Long live the great Chinese People's Liberation Army!" "Long live the great leader Chairman Mao! A long, long life to him!"

The lorry driver, Lo Chang-kuei, was a member of a revolutionary rebel organization. He had been born in a family that suffered bitter oppression before liberation. After the accident, he felt the deepest sorrow and remorse and went to the public security bureau in person to ask for punishment.

When Tso Chia-fa learnt of this, he said to himself: "Not only my wife and daughter, but all proletarian revolutionaries, are near and dear to me. And Comrade Lo Chang-kuei is one of them. Through carelessness he knocked down my wife. But it was a single momentary fault. I should help him draw the lessons from his fault so that he can serve the people better in the future. On no account should I treat a class brother as an enemy".

At home that night Tso sat looking through his wife's copies of the *Selected Works of Mao Tse-tung* and *Quotations From Chairman Mao Tse-tung*. She had read them so often. . . . He was torn with emotion. He recalled Chairman Mao's teaching: **"All people in the revolutionary ranks must care for each other, must love and help each other"**. Suddenly he knew what he should do—he should take these treasured books to Comrade Lo Chang-kuei tomorrow as a gift.

Early the next morning, through the freezing winter air, he went straight to the depot of the Shanghai transport company. The revolutionary staff and workers thronged around and showered expressions of sympathy on him. A meeting was called to "hold high the great red banner of Mao Tse-tung's thought and learn from the People's Liberation Army".

Amidst loud applause, Tso Chia-fa spoke. "Comrades", he said, "I have lost one dear to me and my heart is heavy, but we must not let that affect us in carrying on the struggle against the handful of capitalist roaders inside the Party. Comrade Lo Chang-kuei and other proletarian revolutionaries and I are all revolutionary fighters educated by the great leader Chairman Mao. Army and people, we must unite to form a Great Wall of steel, follow Chairman Mao's great strategic plan closely and carry the great proletarian cultural revolution through to the end". Then he pressed the treasured books into the hands of Lo Chang-kuei and said to him: "Mao Tse-tung's thought is as essential to a revolutionary as the steering wheel is to a driver. My only wish is that you will creatively study and apply Chairman Mao's works, fight self and repudiate revisionism and follow Chairman Mao in making revolution all your life!"

Words failed Lo Chang-kuei. He wept as he embraced Tso Chia-fa. After a long while he said: "I'm grateful to Chairman Mao, grateful to him for bringing up a noble man like you. I'll always remember the lesson I've learnt from this tragic accident, and creatively study and apply Chairman Mao's works. I'll fight self-interest and repudiate revisionism and try to be a model in grasping revolution and promoting production".

The two class brothers, both of whom had suffered deeply in the old society, again fell into slience. Words could not express their deep class feeling for Chairman Mao and for each other. The whole meeting burst into cheers of "Long live Chairman Mao!" and the one thousand people present sang with great emotion,

> Great as are the heavens and earth, what we owe to the
> Party is greater.

Dear as are father and mother, Chairman Mao is dearer.
Fine as many things are, socialism is finer.
Deep as the rivers and oceans are, proletarian love is
*   deeper.*

The next day, Tso Chia-fa and his daughter, the only child, went to see Lo Chang-kuei and gave him a portrait of Chairman Mao.

The whole Lo family was deeply moved. Lo said: "How can I show how grateful I am to you? . . ." Before he had finished, Tso Chia-fa broke in: "Don't thank me but our great leader Chairman Mao who taught me what to do. We are class brothers. We will help each other in the future in the creative study and application of Chairman Mao's works. We must follow Chairman Mao in revolution all our lives".

Gratitude to Chairman Mao filled the hearts of not only the two class brothers, but also of the many neighbours who had heard the story and came to see them.

Peking Review, No. 15, 12 April 1968

CLOSER THAN PARENTS AND CHILDREN

. . . Meantime warning whistles blew, announcing more falling rock and stones, but, defying danger, the members of the shock force came carrying big planks. And as they came they repeated aloud and in unison the quotation: **"Be resolute, fear no sacrifice and surmount every difficulty to win victory"**. A rough shelter was soon built.

Comrade Hsing Kuang-tien shielded Fan Chin's head with his own body. Men united in the thought of Mao Tse-tung feel closer to each other than parents and children. The love of proletarian revolutionary fighters for each other is deeper than the ocean. Even when a big rock fell on Hsing Kuang-tien's helmet, he stayed in position holding up Fan Chin's head. Clenching his teeth as he saw lumps of rock descending the slope uninterruptedly, Hsing Kuang-tien swore to himself never to give in even though the heavens collapsed.

Another landslide came and a wide crack appeared in the emergency shelter. Communist Chen Ta-wen immediately planted his back against the hole. Rocks showered down on his back and shoulders, but he stood firm and protected the shelter from further damage. His action was typical of a man inspired by Chairman Mao's teaching . . .

Peking Review, No. 49, 1 December 1967

A LADLE OF WATER

. . . At night, the temperature on the lake dropped to nearly 30 degrees below zero centigrade. A fresh gale rose, driving snow before it. The 24 commune members, most of them poor and lower-middle peasants, stood on the ice and faced Peking in the snowstorm. They thought of Chairman Mao, who had saved them from the abyss of suffering. They recited aloud Chairman Mao's teaching: **"In times of difficulty we must not lose sight of our achievements, must see the bright future and must pluck up our courage"** and **"be resolute, fear no sacrifice and surmount every difficulty to win victory"**.

As soon as they thought of our great leader Chairman Mao and his brilliant instructions, they became fearless and were full of vigour. Taking Chairman Mao's teachings to heart, they displayed the lofty spirit of class love that Chairman Mao teaches: **"All people in the revolutionary ranks must care for each other,**

must love and help each other".

As it was hard to get drinking water, commune member Chao Yen-lin collected the snow on the ice and used the wooden cases for containing fish as firewood to melt the snow in an iron ladle. The ladle could hold only two or three mouthfuls of water. No one would drink it first. At last all agreed that Li Sheng-kuei, the youngest commune member, should have the first sip. Le Sheng-kuei took only half a mouthful, and then he gave the water to the oldest commune member. In this way eight commune members drank from the ladle, and there was still some left . . .

Peking Radio, 7 March 1969

"IF YOU NEED SKIN, STRIP IT FROM OUR BODIES"

. . . By the time they had corralled the horses, Chang Ching's hands were so cold that he could not open them to release the lasso and reins. The herdsmen and P.L.A. frontier guards ran over to him and carefully removed them from his frozen fingers. One old poor herdsman and a frontier guard rubbed his hands with snow and then put them into a basin of cold water, where two thin "gloves of ice" floated. Bravely bearing the acute pain, Chang Ching kept on asking: "Will my hands still be useful for tending the herds?" The old herdsman unbuttoned his fur-coat to warm the boy's hands and replied with tears in his eyes: "My good boy, you have a red heart, loyal to Chairman Mao. You will certainly be able to tend the herds for us again!" Chang Ching was sent to a frontier guard clinic. Flocking to the clinic, poor and lower-middle herdsmen said to the army doctors: "His hands

73

must be saved. If you need blood, take it from our veins!
If you need skin, strip it from our bodies!" . . .

Peking Radio, 2 March 1969

CLASS BROTHERS

. . . The drivers and conductors always pay special attention to the elderly and handicapped and pregnant women
. . . A woman bus conductor named Tung Ta-lung one
day noticed a passenger waiting at the bus stop who wore
artificial legs and needed somebody to carry him onto the
bus. Tung Ta-lung reminded herself of the following
quotation from Chairman Mao which she used to read
out to the passengers:**"All people in the revolutionary
ranks must care for each other, must love and
help each other"**. Saying "Comrade, let me help you",
she carried the passenger onto the bus and other passengers helped. The handicapped passenger was moved to
tears. He said: "In the old society, the evil capitalist took
away my legs. Chairman Mao and the Communist Party
show me loving care. I came to Peking from the North-
east to have this pair of artificial legs fitted. Class
brothers look after me wherever I go in the capital
where Chairman Mao lives. I will never forget the
goodness of Chairman Mao! A long, long life to Chairman Mao!"

Peking Radio, 6 June 1970

DOING GOOD ALL ONE'S LIFE

. . . After studying the article *In Memory of Norman Bethune* one evening, team member Li Hsiu-jung reviewed her actions in the light of Chairman Mao's teachings. She found that she was deficient in the spirit, as Chairman Mao teaches, of **"utter devotion to others without any thought of self".**

Early the next morning, she went to the home of a paralysed peasant woman names Hsuenh, fetched drinking water, cooked food, and cleaned up for her. Back at home, Li Hsiu-jung studied this teaching of Chairman Mao's: **"It is not hard for one to do a bit of good. What is hard is to do good all one's life and never do anything bad, to act consistently in the interests of the broad masses . . ."** and she decided to go and help every day.

The paralyzed woman was moved to tears and thanked him warmly. Li Hsiu-jung said: "I'm doing this in accordance with Chairman Mao's teachings". From then on, whenever Li Hsiu-jung went to the house, the paralysed woman would shout: "Long live Chairman Mao!" . . .

Peking Radio, 8 March 1969

SAVING THE PATIENT FOR SOCIALIST CONSTRUCTION

. . . Chou Chung-fa, a young worker, was seriously injured by a crane while unloading freight. Rushed to the hospital, his whole body had turned purple and he had great difficulty in breathing. He had a compound fracture of the right collar bone and there was serious internal bleeding of his lungs. The young worker's life was in danger. The medical workers found it hard to treat such a serious case.

The comrades on the worker propaganda team were determined. "We must save him immediately", they said, "even if there's only one chance in a hundred, we must make it a complete success!" The hospital medical personnel were soon organized to save the patient. But the difficulties that cropped up one after another were a serious test for them.

Opening the patient's chest, they found that the right lung had ceased functioning and the left one was bleeding profusely. A heated argument took place in the operating theatre. Most of the surgeons suggested removing the entire right lung. A young surgeon who disagreed said that if the whole right lung were removed the patient would not be able to work after recovery, and this was not right. He proposed excision of only the upper lobe and saving the middle and lower lobes, which possibly could be made to function again. The argument raged on. After carefully listening to the views of both sides, comrades on the propaganda team said that consideration should be given to the question of whether or not the patient could work to serve the socialist revolution and socialist construction in the future. They firmly supported the young surgeon's views.

The operation proved that the decision of the worker propaganda team was correct. The middle and lower lobes of the right lung soon began functioning normally, which helped the patient greatly in his recovery.

In the course of the treatment, the propaganda team arranged for the medical workers to study *In Memory of Norman Bethune* every day to enable them to work wholeheartedly to serve the people. Helped by the team, the medical workers studied *The Foolish Old Man Who Removed the Mountains* to get rid of their fear of difficulties. Their study of *Where Do Correct Ideas Come From?* helped them work out a good plan of treatment. They were able to use Mao Tse-tung thought to analyse their patient's condition and to get hold of the principal contradiction after studying *On Contradiction*. Mao Tse-tung thought guided them in the course of treating the patient. The medical workers used Mao Tse-tung thought to surmount many difficult problems in treating the patient who is now in good health.

This experience was a profound education for the medical personnel. They said: "By relying on invincible Mao Tse-tung thought, the working class can command the scalpel".

Shanghai Radio, 24 July 1969

ROOM AT THE INN

It was a drizzling day. The poor and lower-middle peasants of the Kungchiatun second production team in Kirin Province were sitting around in a circle in a study room, talking away about studying and applying Chairman Mao's works. Suddenly Tsui Fu, the chairman of the brigade's revolutionary committee, entered hurriedly. "There's a woman out on the road about to have her baby!" he exclaimed. "Who can give her a room?"

Everyone fought to invite her to his house. "We can, our family's small", one said. "We have old folk at home to take care of her", others said.

Meanwhile, Fan Yung-ching wanted to have her in his home so much that he sent his daughter home to fix up the house. Then he turned to Tsui Fu and demanded, "Send her to our house, we have plenty of rooms". Tsui Fu accepted.

The woman was Liu Yu-min. It was her first child and, feeling uneasy, she was coming from Heilungkiang province to her sister's home to have the baby. But she had not expected it to come on the way. Her brother-in-law was with her—and very worried, for according to the

77

old custom, to give birth in a stranger's house would bring it bad luck. He did not know what to do. Just then a group of people with raincoats in their hands gathered around Liu Yu-min and took her to Fan Yung-ching's house.

Fan's wife, Cheng Shu-chen, and his daughter Fan Shu-yun had already tidied up. Now they helped carry the woman inside. The midwife arrived. One commune member boiled water, another carried a basin. Soon the baby was born.

It seemed as though everyone was taking part in a happy village event. People were hustling and bustling about in the courtyard. Some brought eggs, others millet. Older women squeezed their way through to help wash and make everything spick and span. As Cheng Shu-chen was busying about, a child yelled from outside, "Aunty, a little chicken fell into your bean-sauce vat!" When she hurried out, her sauce was ruined. No wonder people used to say that a strange birth in the house brings bad luck, she thought. She couldn't help muttering, "How discouraging!" Her movements slowed down. All this was noticed by her daughter Shu-yun.

That evening the family sat down under Chairman Mao's picture to study his works as usual. Shu-yun was the leader and she chose the following quotation for them to study: "**All people in the revolutionary ranks must care for each other, must love and help each other**".

Then she said, "In the old society the landlords used gods and ghosts and such superstition to deceive people. They spread the idea that if a stranger gave birth to a child in one's house it would bring bad luck. Today, in our study group we are going to criticize and repudiate this feudal nonsense".

Fan Yung-ching promptly asked his wife, "What did we call our niece Shu-chin when she was a baby?"

"Chang-ken (Bottom of the Fence)", she replied.

"Why did we call her that?" Then Fan began to tell the story, which happened during the family's suffering before liberation.

"It was winter 1947. The snow was several feet deep. Kuomintang reactionaries were constantly seizing people for their army and robbing the people of their grain. It was impossible to stay home and my sister-in-law had to leave her house to escape trouble. On the way, her baby began to come. It was New Year's Eve and freezing cold. Where could she find a place to have her baby? She begged this family and that, but all the rich people said it would bring them bad luck and they wouldn't let her set foot into their houses.

"All she could find was a low fence to shield her against the bitter north wind and there the child was born. In the piercing wind the baby began to turn blue. Fortunately, she met a woodcutter who took her to his home. In order not to forget that miserable day, she named the baby 'Chang-ken'—Bottom of the Fence".

Shu-yen remarked, "During the great proletarian cultural revolution we got rid of old ideas. We're establishing new proletarian ideas. We shouldn't let feudal superstition come out again to harm people".

All their words hammered at Cheng Shu-chen's heart. Shaken and moved, she said, "Right! The landlords used feudal superstition to deceive and scare us and we shouldn't fall for it".

Early the next morning, Cheng Shu-chen walked into Liu Yu-min's room and said, "Did you hear what I said yesterday? Don't take offence. That was caused by the pernicious feudal influence in me. We will follow Chairman Mao's teaching that once a mistake is made we should correct it". Then she selected some of her largest eggs and cooked them for Yu-min.

Yu-min was moved. Holding Cheng's hand she said, "Aunty, you are closer to me than my own mother. How can I ever thank you?"

Cheng Shu-chen replied, "It's Chairman Mao who has taught me to do this. You should thank him. It's Chairman Mao who's dearest to us all".

Seven days passed and Yu-mins' sister and brother-in-law came to get her. The peasants in the production team came to say goodbye as if seeing off one of their own loved ones. Yu-min's brother-in-law wanted to pay the chairman of the revolutionary committee for the eggs and millet.

"The eggs and millet expressed the feelings and affections of us poor and lower-middle peasants", Tsui Fu answered. "Besides, we don't know who sent these things, so how can we pay anyone?"

Everyone laughed and someone said, "The eggs and millet aren't worth much, it's the class feeling that counts".

Before parting, everybody wanted to suggest a name for the baby. Some said "Yung-hung" (Forever Red). Others suggested "Wei-tung" (Defend Mao Tse-tung). After some thought, Yu-min said, "When the baby arrived it was "meeting people who are boundlessly loyal to Chairman Mao". I think we'd better call it that— "Yu-chung"!"

Gazing at the many new faces which had become so dear to her, tears came to her eyes and Yu-min suddenly shouted, "Long live the victory of the great proletarian cultural revolution! Long live Chairman Mao!"

China Reconstructs, May 1970

Chapter V
Socialist Sacrifice

DEATH AS A LAST AFFIRMATION OF LOYALTY TO CHAIRMAN MAO

... On the day of the cave-in, huge rocks hurtled down on the work face where Hu Ting-ta was working. The lights went out and the tunnel was plunged into darkness. When the roar of the falling rocks died away, the comrades could hear Hu Ting-ta shouting, "Long live Chairman Mao!"

"When we die for the people it is a worthy death". Without a thought for themselves, Liang Yen-hsing and the veteran comrades all rushed towards Hu. They found him lying unconscious, with a broken leg caught between huge rocks pinning his body down. They were about to pull him free when sand and gravel began to fall from the roof of the tunnel. This was the sign of another cave-in. While they remained in the tunnel to save Hu Ting-ta, the veteran comrades asked the young soldier, Liang Yen-hsing, to leave the tunnel quickly.

How good the veteran comrades are! A sudden warmth flooded little Liang's body. "No, I cannot leave. I want to be boundlessly loyal to Chairman Mao, like the veteran comrades!"

He struggled to free himself from the hands trying to push him away from the danger zone and rushed over to little Hu's side, shielding him from the falling rocks with his body. He resolved: "I won't let little Hu get injured again even if it costs me my life!" Little Hu came around briefly to see the golden Chairman Mao badge on Liang Yen-hsing's coat. He said again and again: "Long live Chairman Mao!" Soon after he was taken out of the tunnel, Hu Ting-ta died while saying "Long live Chairman Mao". His last words expressed the boundless love and loyalty of the 60 new fighters for our great leader Chairman Mao.

Peking Radio, 20 April 1969

"FIVE YOUNG PINE TREES"

. . . The names of five heroic teenagers are known far and wide in the rural areas of the northern part of Kiangsi. . . People praise them as "five young pine trees nurtured by Mao Tse-tung thought". Their names are Tsai Ai-tao aged 15, Yen Hung-chih, Wu Kuei-chen, Chi Chu-mao aged 15 and Tsai Chang-li aged 10. These little red soldiers of the Huhsi people's commune in Pengtse County died heroically in the course of putting out a forest fire.

On 28th February 1968, a forest fire suddenly broke out on the Tsaoling Mountain some 1,500 m. from the nearest village. . . The fire swiftly spread. . . Members of the fourth production team of the Hushan brigade of the Huhsi commune were working in the fields at the time. The commune members including the five little red soldiers, raced to the fire . . . After the fire was put out in one spot, the five teenagers immediately plunged into the fight elsewhere, forgetting their fatigue and ignoring the danger.

Tsai Ai-tao's cap caught on fire; Wu Kuei-chen's scarf was burning; Chi Chu-mao's plaits were licked by the flames; and. . . Tsai Chang-li, the youngest of them, was knocked to the ground by a gust of hot air. But the young heroes fought unflinchingly. . . and the fire was finally put out.

But smouldering ashes at the bottom of the valley flared up and instantly the fire rose and in seconds became raging flames. The five youngsters again joined the other commune members in the fight to cut out the fire. People saw them run into the flames and heard them recite Chairman Mao's great teaching: **"when we die for the people it is a worthy death"**. In an instant, the five young heroes were surrounded by the conflagration, but people still heard shouts of "Long live Chairman Mao!" loud and clear. . . The young heroes went on fighting, heedless of the danger.

At last the fire was extinguished and the collective property was saved, but the five young heroes had laid down their lives.

Through their daily work and labour, they consciously trained themselves and fostered the spirit of fearing neither hardship nor death. They were nurtured by Mao Tse-tung thought and with their young lives wrote a song of victory in praise of Mao Tse-tung thought.

NCNA, 30 May 1970

DYING FOR COLLECTIVE SHEEP

An elderly former poor peasant couple, Chang Chi-jung and his wife, in Yenkuan people's commune, Kansu Province, gave up their lives in an effort to save a flock of the commune's sheep. They have set a shining example in defending the collective economy and consolidating the socialist state.

The revolutionary committee in Lihsien County, where the people's commune is located, posthumously awarded Comrade Chang Chi-jung the title of "Commune member boundlessly loyal to Chairman Mao".

. . . At midnight on 21 April this year, Chang Chi-jung

fell asleep after discussing with his wife and 13-year-old daughter, Chun-Hua, how to further carry out Chairman Mao's policy to **"grasp revolution and promote production"** and how to take an active part in the revolutionary mass repudiation. Suddenly, a huge roar awoke the family. They concluded that the heavy spring rains must have caused the cave used as the sheep shelter to crumble. Chang Chi-jung quickly went to the cave with a shovel. His wife and daughter also hurried along with an oil lamp. A layer of mud had fallen from the ceiling of the cave and 29 sheep were buried. There were only the three of them in the dark cave.

Lumps of mud continued to fall from the ceiling. Greater danger awaited them. Chang Chi-jung recalled Chairman Mao's teaching: **"Be resolute, fear no sacrifice and surmount every difficulty to win victory"**. He told his wife: "Hurry up, save the sheep, save the sheep. We cannot allow any damage to the socialist cause!" The couple rushed further into the cave disregarding the danger. The cave was lighted by the oil lamp which the daughter held. The crevices in the ceiling grew bigger and bigger and a cave-in was possible at any moment. To encourage his wife at such a crucial time, Chang Chi-jung very calmly recited aloud Chairman Mao's teaching: **"So long as a single man remains, he will fight on"**.

At this moment, they heard a lamb bleating. Brimming with joy, he said to his wife: "So long as I remain alive, the collective sheep will not die". Suddenly the ceiling crumbled completely. Villagers came up the mountain in haste. When they dug away the thick layer of earth, Chang Chi-jung and his wife had already been smothered. Only the daughter at the door was alive. The villagers were grieved over the loss of their comrades in arms. They recalled that Chang Chi-jung had been active in collective production. They said this hero would always remain alive in their hearts.

Peking Radio, 28 June 1968

A MARTYR'S DIARY

. . . Comrade Chin Hsun-hua was a 1968 graduate of the senior class of the Wusung No. 2 high school of Shanghai municipality. He is from a worker's family and was a former member of the standing committee of the Shanghai Red Guard congress of middle schools. In the course of the great proletarian cultural revolution he closely followed Chairman Mao's great strategic plan and plunged into the fierce struggle to smash the bourgeois headquarters headed by the renegade, hidden traitor and scab Liu Shao-chi.

In May 1969, responding to the great leader Chairman Mao's call, **"Educated young people should go to the countryside and accept re-education by the poor and lower-middle peasants"**, he took the lead in settling down at the Shuangho production brigade, Hsunho commune, Hsunko County, Heilungkiang Province.

On 15 August 1969, floodwater poured down from both sides of the Shuang River. To save state materials Chin Hsun-hua unfortunately but gloriously sacrificed his life. In accordance with the repeated requests by Comrade Chin before his death, the party organization concerned admitted him posthumously as a member of the CCP . . .

Excerpts from Comrade Chin Hsun-hua's diary (July-August 1969)

1 July

Today is the 48th birthday of the great, glorious, and correct Community Party of China. It is the Party and Chairman Mao that have educated me and transformed me from an ignorant boy to a grown man. It is as a result of the great leader Chairman Mao's education that I have been able to grow up.

O Party! Your little red soldier will always closely

follow you to march forward. I pledge that while transforming the objective world, I will do my best to remould my world outlook ideologically and organizationally in the vast expanse of the countryside so that I may join the great, glorious, and correct Communist Party of China as soon as possible, closely follow our great leader Chairman Mao, and wage a strenuous life-time struggle so as to realize communism throughout the whole world.

Here I want to pledge to the Party once again: I will strictly demand of myself to behave in accordance with the criteria of a Communist Party member and act in the spirit of the new constitution of the Party so that I may join the Communist Party of China at an early date.

Long live the Communist Party of China! Long live the great leader Chairman Mao, a long, long life to him!

2 July

My work today was to put the straw in bundles. I was not very good at it. When I had tied only a few bundles, I cut my hands and they bled. I intended to take a rest but at that time I recalled Chairman Mao's teaching: **"It is very necessary for educated young people to go to the countryside to be re-educated by the poor and lower-middle peasants"**. My hands bled but not the hands of the poor and lower-middle peasants. This indicates that my hands as well as my thoughts have been divorced from the workers, peasants and labour for a long time and are stained with the poison of revisionism. They should be tempered through protracted labour with the masses of workers and peasants.

Seeing my trouble, the poor and lower-middle peasants patiently taught me how to tie the bundles. By following Chairman Mao's instruction to look upon the poor and lower-middle peasants as teachers, I quickly picked up the skill and carried on the work energetically.

This means that we educated young people should be re-educated by the poor and lower-middle peasants in the three great revolutionary movements, change the wavering and vacillating nature of the petty bourgeois intellectuals, and carry the revolution through to the end . . .

4 July

Now I began to realize the acute and violent nature of the class struggle in the countryside. . . I, a Red Guard o Chairman Mao's, have made every preparation to use invincible Mao Tse-tung thought to deal the reactionary forces a direct blow. I am willing even to sacrifice [my life] if necessary. Try to fight for the sake of the consolidation of the proletarian dictatorship! Fight! Fight! . . .

10 July

I am a member of the new generation of Chinese youth and one of Chairman Mao's Red Guards who have been steeled for three years in the great proletarian cultural revolution. I have already made up my mind to go to the frontier area of the fatherland to oppose imperialism and revisionism, conscientiously accept re-education by the poor and lower-middle peasants, and carry the socialist revolution through to the end . . .

11 July

Yesterday a comrade wrote me a letter and told me that newspapers in Shanghai had carried a news report about me and several other standing committee members of the Shanghai Red Guard congress of middle schools.

I do not know what was said in the news report. Anyway, I know this much: it is not my own achievement alone. It is the result of Chairman Mao's education, a victory for Mao Tse-tung thought. I am determined to follow Chairman Mao's teachings: **"Be modest and prudent, guard against arrogance and impetuosity"**, and march forward all the time. March on,

Chairman Mao's Red Guards! . . .

16 July

Yesterday was the third anniversary of our great leader Chairman Mao's swim in the Yangtze River. Our great leader Chairman Mao is in such excellent health; this is the greatest happiness for the revolutionary people in China and the whole world. Let us shout at the top of our voices a thousand, ten thousand times: Long live Chairman Mao! A long, long life to him!

Under the leadership of our great leader Chairman Mao, and under the guidance of Mao Tse-tung thought, let us advance courageously in the new high tide of the world revolution and in the storms and waves of the class struggle both in China and in the world. Following Chairman Mao means victory!

In the afternoon, I had a pain in my stomach. I thought I might as well not go to work. But then I remembered that now production work is very pressing and we are very short of manpower. It might seem unimportant for one man to be absent from work, but the effect would be bad on the others. Then, while I was working, I found my stomach pain was not so serious after all.

This shows that the young people, particularly young intellectuals, can relieve some of their illnesses by doing productive labour. We can rid ourselves of our physical weaknesses while transforming our ideology. I am determined to transform my own body while transforming my ideology . . .

20 July

This afternoon, I went for a swim in the river. As I stood on the bank I saw that the current was very swift. Shall I swim? The current is really frightening, I thought to myself. At this juncture, I remembered Chairman Mao's teaching: **"Even big storms and waves are not**

formidable. It is precisely amid storms and waves that human society develops". Knowing that a man can cultivate bravey and toughness in the swift current, I jumped into the river and swam a score of metres.

This has borne out the truth: If a man has strong revolutionary will and can study well, he can overwhelm the current, no matter how swift it is. If a Chinese youth is armed with Mao Tse-tung thought and constantly follows Chairman Mao closely, he can pass through swift currents and dangerous shoals . . .

23 July

The poor and lower-middle peasants are our best teachers in giving us re-education because they are the most loyal to Chairman Mao. As soon as Chairman Mao's latest instruction on consolidating Party organization—which was made known in the joint editorial carried by the *People's Daily*, the *Red Flag*, and the *Liberation Army Daily* —reached us, with boundless loyalty to Chairman Mao, we paid a house-to-house visit to the poor and lower-middle peasants to disseminate the latest instruction.

It was quite late in the evening when we arrived at Grandma Sung's house. She had already gone to bed. As soon as she learned that Chairman Mao's latest instruction had been published, she immediately jumped out of bed and politely accepted a copy of the instruction. After lighting a kerosene lamp, she woke up every member of the family and they immediately began to study the instruction.

We were really moved by this scene. It is clear to what extent the poor and lower-middle peasants are loyal to Chairman Mao! When we started to disseminate the latest instruction, we were worried about what to do if the poor and lower-middle peasants would not accept us because it was so late in the evening. What a fine contrast! . . .

24 July

The gun is the main prop of political power. I am determined to arm myself with Mao Tse-tung thought, actively to devote efforts to the struggle to defend Chairman Mao, to live to fight for Chairman Mao's revolutionary line, and to die gloriously defending it.

25 July

Recently I was asked to participate in the performance of literary and art programmes. This really put me in a dilemma. It is my bound duty to disseminate Mao Tse-tung thought, but I do not know anything about acting. What if there are flaws in my performance? I then studied Chairman Mao's works. By studying, my mind became clear. With a clear mind, I learned relatively well and in a short time I mastered some of the fundamentals of acting.

I should use literature and art as a medium of disseminating Mao Tse-tung thought, and I am determined to serve the poor and lower-middle peasants well. The young intellectuals in the rural areas should do the same . . .

28 July

We must be strict with ourselves and lenient with our comrades. Every little achievement I have scored has been under the guidance of Chairman Mao's brilliant thought. Since I am a correspondent, I must devote my energy to the work of propagating heroic deeds in my area, conscientiously learn from the anonymous heroes, sincerely be the workhorse of the people, and diligently serve the poor and lower-middle peasants for my entire life.

29 July

After studying Chairman Mao's brilliant work *Report on an Investigation of the Peasant Movement in Hunan*, I began to understand that Chairman Mao gave a high mark to the peasant movement. It came to my mind that I have already been working in the rural areas for almost two months. And what is my attitude toward the poor and lower-middle peasants? There are still old ideologies in my mind. Sometimes I even think that I came to the countryside as an "official". If this idea is allowed to develop, I shall soon be sitting on the shoulders of the poor and lower-middle peasants and ordering them about.

It is necessary to use Mao Tse-tung thought to thoroughly criticize and discredit this sort of poisonous idea and to master Chairman Mao's teaching in his *Report on an Investigation of the Peasant Movement in Hunan*: **"Leadership by the poor peasants is absolutely necessary. Without the poor peasants there would be no revolution. To deny their role is to deny the revolution, to attack the revolution"** . . .

1 August

On 1 August, Army Day, the joint editorial "The People's Liberation Army Is Invincible Everywhere", carried by the *People's Daily*, the *Red Flag*, and the *Liberation Army Daily*, brought to us Chairman Mao's instruction: **"I am for the slogan 'Fear neither hardship nor death'."** In the past I have always believed that I performed well in the great proletarian cultural revolution. Even though I have not made any contribution, I have worked hard and suffered physical fatigue. This sort of thinking has remained quite strong in my mind. Although I have subjected it to criticism on several occasions, its poisonous influence has not been thoroughly eliminated.

Chairman Mao's latest instructions fell on me like a

heavy shell and brought me to my senses. My ideas on merit run exactly counter to Chairman Mao's teachings. This way of thinking must be criticized. Only thus can we foster the proletarian concept of fearing neither hardship nor death and understand the viewpoint of happiness and suffering, and advance along the road of revolution with greater efforts . . .

6 August

An evening meeting was held, sharply to criticize Liu Shao-chi's "theory of the dying out of the class struggle". Vivid facts on class struggle remind us that the class struggle is far from over. Some demons of a certain production brigade were always attempting a counter-attack in retaliation. A certain counter-revolutionary had engaged in sabotage in the middle of the night. When he was captured by the militia, he threatened the masses of people by saying that he would commit suicide.

Reconciled to their defeat, the surviving class enemies still try to recapture at all times the paradise they have lost . . .

7 August

Last night rain fell while a meeting was in progress. We immediately stopped our meeting and woke up the militia on duty to pick up clay bricks lying outside. With help from many persons, the clay bricks were moved inside. We were very happy after the work was done. This can be considered as a vivid example of receiving re-education from poor and lower-middle peasants.

10 August

Worked on a plot of barley this morning. It occurred to me in the afternoon that working on something else would be much easier. After working on this plot of land, I again felt that collecting wheat is more relaxing than this. This fact indicates that if one's mind is not occupied by Chairman Mao's thought, it will of course be occupied by bourgeois ideology; as a result, one would take the easy work and be afraid of arduous tasks, and would avoid undergoing ideological transformation. I am determined to carry on the study, arm my mind with Mao Tse-tung thought, and march forward unceasingly.

12 August

A meeting was held this morning to criticize anarchism. Anarchism finds expression in: being late for work and leaving early; being absent without reason; refusing to criticize; playing cards or chess while on duty; undermining unity; and undermining proletarian discipline.

Every comrade attending the meeting unanimously criticized this reactionary ideological trend. I am determined to observe strict proletarian discipline and to strive to become a model in observing party discipline.

13 August

Talked of the problem of lamps and have come to a conclusion: No matter how bright the lamp is, when one's ideology is dark, one still feels the lamp is dark. No matter how small the wick is, whenever I study Chairman Mao's works, my heart feels bright all over. The more I study, the more I feel this way. It is because Mao Tse-tung thought lights the direction for our advance.

14 August (The day before his sacrifice)

Today heard the note delivered by our Foreign Ministry from a broadcast: I am so angry. Chairman Mao teaches us: **"We must never be cowed by the bluster of reactionaries"**. The 700 million soldiers and people of China are waiting to meet the enemies in full battle array and to deal a resolute blow to the aggressors. We would like to warn imperialism, revisionism, and reactionaries:

the revolutionary youth in the era of Mao Tse-tung thought are not to be trifled with. If U.S. imperialism and Soviet revisionist social-imperialism dare to try to invade, then they will run into the iron fist of the third and fourth generations of China!

We are the youth of a new generation in socialist China. It is sheer fantasy for U.S. imperialism and Soviet revisionism to pin their hopes of restoring capitalism on us! Since we have smashed the corrosion of the bourgeois ideology, why should we be afraid of you paper tigers armed to the teeth!

Down with U.S. imperialism!
Down with social-imperialism!
Vow to safeguard the territory of the motherland!
Vow to defend Mao Tse-tung thought!
Vow to defend Chairman Mao!

Peking Radio, 3 December 1969

MARTYR POSTHUMOUSLY RECEIVED INTO THE PARTY

. . . In April 1965 Comrade Hsieh Chen-hsin risked his life and succeeded in saving a son of a poor peasant from a fire. On 17 May 1968 Comrade Hsieh Chen-hsin, aware of the dangers of an electric shock, saved the life of commune member Li Chi-nien by absorbing the shock himself. Sacrificing himself, he rescued this class brother and also saved other poor and lower-middle peasants from death. He fulfilled his iron-clad oath always to be loyal to Chairman Mao and to fear no difficulties or sacrifices in making revolution, as well as to be a willing pupil of poor and lower-middle peasants.

It is hereby decided that Comrade Hsieh Chen-hsin be posthumously declared a member of the Chinese Communist Party and a revolutionary marytr.

Hofei, Anhwei Provincial broadcast, 24 December 1969

"SACRIFICE OF THE FEW IS THE COST OF HAPPINESS FOR THE MANY"

. . . Four of our comrades-in-arms gloriously gave their lives in the struggle against the almost non-stop series of rock-falls. In a blood-stained pocket of hero Liu Kuo-lu, inside a copy of *Quotations From Chairman Mao Tse-tung*, was a piece of paper—inserted as a bookmark—before the chapter "Dare to Struggle and Dare to Win". Neatly written on the paper were the words: **"The sacrifice of the few is the cost of happiness for the many"**. These moving words voiced the common feeling deep in the hearts of all the martyrs who were determined to live and die for the people . . .

Peking Review, No. 49, 1 December 1967

"IF YOU WANT TO KNOW THE TASTE OF A PEAR"

. . . One day, Yu Chung-hsiang, a patient with a secondary cataract, came to the medical team for treatment. Since 1958 he had been to well-known doctors and specialists in hospitals in several big cities for treatment. Because these bourgeois authorities had no class feeling for the labouring people, they treated the patient irresponsibly and Yu Chung-hsiang's eyes became worse, and at last he lost his sight.

After being assigned the task of treating him, Chen Chi-chin searched through data on acupuncture but could find no example of a cataract being removed. Spurred on by the desire to rid his class brother of his anguish, he was determined to blaze a trail. He studied Chairman Mao's teaching: **"if you want knowledge, you must take part in the practice of changing reality. If you want to know the taste of a pear, you must change the pear by eating it yourself"**. Standing in front of a mirror, he experimented on his own eyes. He inserted the needle beyond a depth of five fen, the limit set by books on acupuncture.

As he was doing this, he felt that he might go blind. But this teaching of Chairman Mao's instantly came to mind: **"Countless revolutionary martyrs have laid down their lives in the interests of the people, and our hearts are filled with pain as we, the living, think of them—can there be any personal interest, then, that we would not sacrifice or any error that we would not discard?"**

He thought of Doctor Bethune, a foreigner who gave his life for the liberation of the Chinese people. Why, he asked himself, could he not sacrifice one of his eyes for a class brother? He made up his mind that even if it cost him his own sight he would restore the patient's eyesight.

After dozens of insertions at different depths at the inner corners of his eyes he finally became experienced in inserting the needles in various areas of the eyes. After 10 treatments, Yu Chung-hsiang was able to see Chairman Mao's portrait on the wall. The patient jumped up and, with tears in his eyes, cheered in happiness: "Long live Chairman Mao!"

As a result of summing up their experience and creating new experience, the medical team has cured many cases of blindness due to glaucoma, optic atrophy, and extreme near-sightedness . . .

Peking Radio, 19 March 1969

SELF-EFFACING HERO

. . . Hearing the news of the accident, people quickly came to the hospital and expressed their willingness to donate blood for a transfusion. A large number of people wrote letters to comfort Ning Hsueh-chin. Local newspapers, radio stations, and the television station reported his deeds. The Party was much concerned about him. In his ward, big-character posters—"Learn from the Wang Chien-type hero" and "Learn from the communist fighter who is like Tsai Yung-hsiang"—were seen on the wall.

Ning Hsueh-chin felt very uneasy about the praise given him by the Party and people. He said: "Chairman Mao, Oh Chairman Mao! All I have was given by you. You liberated me from the stick of the landlords. I have grown up nurtured by your brilliant thought. Although my skin was broken here and there and I lost some drops of blood, it is nothing! It is far, far less than the Party's concern for me and your training given to me. I will live up to your expectations. So long as I live, I will struggle endlessly to defend your revolutionary line and to liberate mankind!"

Peking Radio, 13 July 1969

RED WOMEN ROUSE SEAMEN

Five female members of a worker propaganda team stationed at the Shanghai Sea Transport Bureau have been working on the Chinese Ship Chantou No. 24. Their determination to do a good job despite strong winds, turbulent waves, and seasickness has won them the title of "Red detachment of women on the sea".

On their first voyage, the ship ran into strong winds. Although they were vomiting they still carried on their work, propagating Mao Tse-tung thought among the passengers and seamen. When vibrations from the pounding waves ripped out one of the ship's pumps, the women ran to the navigation room reading quotations from Chairman Mao to the seamen and criticizing Liu Shao-chi's "philosophy of survival". Inspired by these brave women, the sailors risked their lives and repaired the broken pipe, thus saving the ship from mortal peril.

Shanghai Radio, 18 October 1969

Chapter VI

Guilt and Confession

REACHING THE DEPTHS OF THEIR SOULS

... To cope with the situation, the leading group responsible for the rectification and building of the Party, and the P.L.A. support-the-left personnel, educated the party members on the aims of conducting "combat self and repudiate revisionism" work, particularly in ridding themselves of bourgeois ideas, promoting their understanding of Mao Tse-tung thought, and further enhancing their class consciousness and consciousness of the struggle between the two lines. The leading group and the P.L.A. personnel urged the party members to take Chairman Mao's programme for party building as their guiding principle, combat self in the very depth of their souls, and thoroughly repudiate revisionism.

A number of party members, who were misled ideologically by the book on self-cultivation, did not know the political orientation of how to be a proletarian vanguard fighter. Consequently they were unable to reach the very depths of their souls. A small number of others, who knew the political orientation, did not intend to do so because they were afraid of hurting their souls.

The leading group and the P.L.A. personnel first of all led the masses of party members in carrying out the "two recollections" and "two check-ups" activities: they recalled the history of the struggle between the two lines within the plant and analysed their own performance in the struggle, and recalled the C.C.P.'s role in the Chinese revolution and world revolution and analysed disputed points with the proletarian vanguard fighters.

This led the party members to engage themselves

in the struggle between the two lines, analyse their own views and attitudes in the various historical stages, particularly in the three-year great proletarian cultural revolution, and identify the key issues.

A party member, a cadre misled by the big renegade Liu Shao-chi's fallacy "join the Party to be an official", closely followed the capitalist-roaders in the plant in an attempt to gain a higher position. He was called an "official cretin" by the masses. In carrying out "combat self and repudiate revisionism", he listed his past mistakes and his shortcomings and fought himself repeatedly. However, the masses were not satisfied because he failed to touch the very depth of his soul.

Later, the leading group and the masses helped him study hard Chairman Mao's programme for rectifying and building the Party and carry out the "two recollections" and "two check-ups" activities. Through recalling his own activities in the various political movements, he realized that he was taking the dangerous road of "joining the Party to be an official". Eventually he clarified his erroneous thinking and touched the very depth of his soul. Having grasped the key problem, he got rid of the stale from the depth of his soul, conducted self-criticism conscientiously, and swiftly enhanced his consciousness of the struggle between the two lines.

Another party member seldom participated in political activities. He always sat in the rear at meetings and never expressed his views. His labour discipline was quite slack. When the rectification of the Party began, the masses decided that he must rid himself of the stale during the campaign. He also knew that his problem was serious.

The leading group responsible for rectification and party-building analysed his case conscientiously, found that he was infected by Liu Shao-chi's fallacies, and aroused the masses to help him clarify his position at meetings and rid himself of the stale and to hold individual talks at his home. This helped him realize that he was wrong by taking the dangerous road of peaceful evolution. When this key issue was grasped, he fought self consciously and intensely repudiated revisionism. He spoke in self-criticism only once at a meeting, but the masses unanimously agreed to accept his confession. He was not urged to withdraw from the Party. His confession also educated other party members . . .

. . . To avoid having party members recall their past mistakes behind closed doors, the Shenyang metallurgical plant has comprehensively carried out heart-to-heart talks and organized the "with one helping another, a pair will become Red" activities among party members and between party members and the masses. To avoid letting anyone get out of a tight spot easily, the plant pays special attention to achieving effectiveness by eliminating formalism. In fighting self the "combat self and repudiate revisionism" meeting is not the only place where party members may be examined and criticized by others.

If necessary, party members may make self-criticism under any circumstances if it is helpful in "getting rid of the stale and letting in the fresh" ideologically, or helpful in strengthening the combat force of party members. The majority of party members of the plant have fought self at the forums for the living study and application of Mao Tse-tung thought or at criticism meetings.

Shenyang, Liaoning Provincial Broadcast, 1 November 1969

VEXED BY UNCLEAN SPIRITS

One night in April this year an old comrade of about 50 years of age was paying his respects to Chairman Mao's picture together with his family. This was Comrade Chang Shih-chun, formerly deputy director of the

Industrial Publishing Agency of the Scientific and Technological Commission of the State Council and party committee deputy secretary. With the patient and meticulous help of the P.L.A. support-the-left personnel stationed at the agency, the worker-P.L.A.-Mao Tse-tung thought propaganda team, and the revolutionary masses, he returned to the side of Chairman Mao's revolutionary line and was liberated.

Several months ago at a meeting, the question of liberating Chang Shih-chun was brought up and a debate ensued. Some held that "he had for a long time carried out the big renegade Liu Shao-chi's counter-revolutionary revisionist line, that he had again carried out the bourgeois reactionary line during the great proletarian cultural revolution, and that his mistakes were too serious". But the majority felt that he should be educated and liberated. They organized a study class to help him. After some time some comrades lost confidence in him for he failed to come round. The P.L.A. men and the propaganda team organized the masses to study Chairman Mao's policy and gave Chang Shih-chun more help. They found that his difficulty was that he thought that the masses were against him, because another cadre who had committed even more serious mistakes had been liberated before him. The comrades held many talks with him for more than two months, and his understanding slowly showed some progress. The comrades then made a concerted effort to help him overcome his self-interest. Finally, Chang Shih-chun made a soul-searching self-examination and he was declared liberated.

Peking Radio, 28 June 1969

BARING ONE'S SELF-INTEREST

Last spring the family of Chen Chung-ying, a poor peasant of the No. 1 production team, held a study class with all seven members of his family participating. Soon there appeared a problem: "Inadequate combat against self-interest and half-hearted repudiation of revisionism". Shang ho-ching, husband of Chen Chung-ying, remained silent in the class. In the classes held at the production team he spoke not a single word for three days. When his wife discovered this, she asked what kind of classes had been held in the production brigade. He said: "In the classes they wanted us to combat self-interest. What self-interest have I to combat? There is really no self-interest to combat!"

In 1962 the evil wind of "three freedoms and one contract" came to Chilaotien. At that time the five children of Chen Chung-ying were still small and his wife was always sick. They had a hard time. Incited by the class enemies, he did something detrimental to the collective interest. Because of self-interest, this matter remained secret. One night when the family gathered in front of Chairman Mao's picture to combat self-interest and repudiate revisionism Chen Chung-ying said: "Chairman Mao wants us to combat self-interest and repudiate revisionism. If we do not lay bare our self-interest, how can we look Chairman Mao in the face?"

The 12-year-old son said: "Right! If you do not wipe away the dirt of self-interest how can you follow Chairman Mao in making revolution?" Two days later the husband decided to tell all in the study class held at the production brigade. However, while he was trying to expose his crime, self-interest reared its ugly head and as a result he held something back. With indignation, his wife returned home before the meeting ended. As soon as the husband returned, she asked: "Have you bared your self-interest?" He said, "Yes". She replied bluntly: "Chairman Mao has taught us not to forget class struggle. You failed to expose the class enemies and you bared only half of your self-interest. As a cadre of the production brigade how can you make revolution with self-interest in your mind?" The husband replied: "If I bared too much, I would be ashamed to meet people".

The son immediately criticized him for not having thoroughly bared his self-interest. The son said: "We poor and lower-middle peasants can never tell lies before Chairman Mao's picture. Chairman Mao has taught us: **"Mistakes are inevitable: it will be well if we seriously correct them"**. If you lay bare your self interest, you should not feel ashamed. The scoundrel, China's Khrushchev, has tried to lead us into the dead end of capitalism so that we would have to take a second dose of misery. You must never be deceived".

The husband was greatly moved. He said: "I have forgotten myself. I must apologize to Chairman Mao. I must make a complete break with self-interest". Later he went all out to expose the crimes of class enemies at the class session and thoroughly exposed his own self-interest. His action was greatly welcomed by everybody.

Through the study classes, the theory of "the dying out of class struggle" by China's Khrushchev has been strongly repudiated in this production brigade. The political consciousness of class struggle and the struggle between the two lines has been greatly enhanced. Chang Kuo-hai, a 10-year old boy, is most enthusiastic in the struggle against enemies and particularly hates the class enemies taking advantage of clan authority to make trouble. His grandfather told the people: "Whenever my grandson sees me he shouts about striking me down". The mother of the child said seriously, "He is right. You have done evil things and deserve to be struck down".

Because of the merits of family study classes in Mao Tse-tung's thought, the poor and lower-middle peasants are all saying: "Before, the family was a haven of self-interest; now it is the front line for combating self-interest".

Tsinan, Shantung Provincial Broadcast, 20 August 1968

RECANTING FATHER

... Chi Jen-fu's family is made up of six persons. He used to have the final word in all family affairs. Even at production team meetings, Chi Jen-fu's children dared not speak if the old man was present. Chi Shu-chin, the second daughter, became a revolutionary path-breaker soon after the great cultural revolution began. She was elected an activist in the study of Chairman Mao's works. Chi Jen-fu had a hard time enforcing his patriarchal attitude.

Outside the family, Chi Jen-fu tried not to say very much because he found Chi Shu-chin's arguments sounder and more effective than his. But in the family he insisted his daughter must obey him. Thus there were frequent contradictions between him and his daughter.

At one production team meeting Chi Shu-chin suggested that the method of recording work points daily be changed to one which put proletarian politics to the fore, like that of the Tachai brigade. Under that method, the work of a commune member was translated into work points only once a year. In addition to the amount of labour, the commune member's political attitude, his approach toward work, and the quality of his labour were also important factors. This move won the approval of all present except Chi Jen-fu, who didn't utter a word. Back at home that night, Chi Shu-chin said: "Father, why didn't you speak at the meeting?" Chi Jen-fu said coldly: "If you want me to speak, you must first withdraw your suggestion". Chi Shu-chin smiled, saying, "Withdraw? On the contrary, our family must take the lead in carrying it out". All of a sudden, Chi Jen-fu flew into a rage, declaring: "Outside the family, we all obey you. But in the family, you must obey me. This is family custom. What's wrong with the recording of work points every day? The more one works, the more one gets. That has always been the practice".

Chi Shu-chin could not sleep that night. She thought that if the struggle-criticism-transformation was to be successful in the production team, it must first be done successfully in the family. She made up her mind to do away with all out-of-date habits and customs in the family and place Mao Tse-tung's thought in command of the family. At the family study class the next evening Chi Shu-chin led the whole family in studying this quotation from Chairman Mao: **"The force at the core leading our cause forward is the Chinese Communist Party. The theoretical basis guiding our thinking is Marxism-Leninism"**. Then she asked her father: "You just brought up the principle that 'he who works more gets more', but in the old society the toiling masses worked day and night and still led a miserable life. Why?"

These words hit Chi Jen-fu where it hurt most and reminded him of the sufferings of the past. He said with clenched fists: "I know that very well. It is all because we did not have political power". Chi Shu-chin added: "You are right! Chairman Mao teaches: **'The fundamental question of revolution is political power'**. But is it right that now we have political power we should work only in order to get more? No, father. If we work to get more work points, we may for a time earn more grain and money, but at the same time we may forget to consolidate the dictatorship of the proletariat, which is the heart of the matter. If we did that, our heads might be cut off without our even knowing the reason. We are now adopting the Tachai method in recording work points. We are doing this to give prominence to proletarian politics and establish the concept of farming for the revolution".

Chi Jen-fu thought over his daughter's remarks and remembered Chairman Mao's teaching: **"Only socialism can save China"**. His heart was suddenly light and he exclaimed: "I was poisoned by Liu Shao-chi's 'put work points in command!' " He then pledged to take a lead in responding to Chairman Mao's call: **"In agriculture learn from Tachai"** and to carry out the Tachai method.

When the family fight-self-and-repudiate-revisionism

meeting was about to end, Chi Shu-chin's younger brother jumped up and said: "What Shu-chin did today is correct. From now on, she should be in charge of the family". The father and mother agreed to this. But Shu-chin said: "No, you are wrong. From now on we listen only to the one whose idea conforms with the thought of Mao Tse-tung, whether the person is young or old, man or woman". Everyone was satisfied and said: "Good! Mao Tse-tung's thought should command our family life!"

One evening, Chi Jen-fu's family was studying Chairman Mao's great teachings that **"You should concern yourselves with affairs of state and carry through the great proletarian cultural revolution to the end"** and that the peasants **"should also criticize the bourgeoisie"**. Chi Jen-fu said: "Revolutionary mass criticism and repudiation is part of Chairman Mao's strategic plan. It is an affair of state. We have made it a rule to 'place Mao Tse-tung's thought in command of our family life'. From now on, we must make it another rule of our family to repudiate Liu Shao-chi every day". Since then, the whole family, young and old, has repudiated the towering crimes of Liu Shao-chi every day, and turned its home into a battleground of revolutionary mass criticism and repudiation.

Peking Radio, 10 January 1969

REFORMED SON SHOULDERS BURDEN

. . . When Mai Hsien-yu was elected a member of the standing committee of the Jaoping County Revolutionary Committee and concurrently chairman of the conference of representatives of the poor and lower-middle peasants of the same county, he was hesitant. He worried that he would not measure up to the heavy burden entrusted to him because he had had only a very limited opportunity in education and he lacked experience. His father, Mai A-chi, soon discovered what was on his mind.

Being aware of Mai Hsien-yu's prevailing frame of mind, his father, A-chi, organised the whole family one evening earnestly to study Chairman Mao's teachings on serving the people and on building state power. During the study session, his voice full of emotion, he said affectionately: "Son, you must never forget the miserable life that was the lot of us poor and lower-middle peasants in the old society. You must never forget how much we are indebted to our great liberator Chairman Mao!" He was followed by the son's 78-year-old grandmother who said: "Power was not easily won in the old society, it was precisely because the seal of power was not in the hands of the poor and lower-middle peasants that your father and mother, with your newly born elder brother in a basket, were forced to flee to Fukien Province to save their lives, and that your uncle died of starvation in front of our door. . . ."

In a voice that showed her emotion, sister Mai Hsien-mei said: "It is thanks to Chairman Mao that we, a family who lived on a boat and were brought up in misery, are now taking part in the work of the revolutionary committees at various levels. We must act in accordance with Chairman Mao's instructions and take firm hold of the seal of proletarian power".

Chairman Mao's teachings greatly enlightened Mai Hsien-yu, and the words of the father and sister and reminiscences of the miserable past and deep appreciation of the happy present made by his grandmother gave him a new understanding. He said: "Poor and lower-middle peasants have confidence in me for the sole reason of entrusting me with the task of doing well at assuming power for the proletariat. But considerations of 'self' made me shrink from shouldering the heavy burden".

He then made a penetrating criticism of his egoistic inclinations before members of the family and said he was determined to do his best to shoulder the task. Before the study session adjourned, Mai A-chi led the whole family to stand before the portrait of Chairman Mao and made the following solemn vow: "There are a thousand and one requirements, but the living study and application of Mao Tse-tung thought is the primary requirement; there may be a thousand and one changes, but the Red hearts devoted to Chairman Mao will never change; there are a thousand and one roads, but it is the revolutionary road indicated by Chairman Mao that must be followed. We pledge ourselves to take good hold of power and wield it well for the proletariat and the poor and lower-middle peasants. We pledge ourselves to dedicate our Red hearts to the people".

Our great leader Chairman Mao teaches: **"We should never divorce ourselves from the masses. Only in this way are we able to know them, understand them and be one with them, and are we able to serve the people well".** This brilliant instruction of Chairman Mao's pointed out the orientation for Mai Hsien-te's family most clearly.

Peking Radio, 31 October 1969

EXORCISING EXPERTISE

. . . The propaganda team ran many Mao Tse-tung thought study classes in the hospital to help the intellectuals make a living study and application of Chairman Mao's three constantly read articles and in judging themselves repeatedly in the light of the communist spirit of fearing neither hardship nor death. This touched them to the core of their being. Many of the intellectuals criticized their bourgeois ideas such as "seeking money and fame", "putting technique in the first place" and "knowledge is private property". A doctor, who had been poisoned by the revisionist line into doing his utmost to study technique used to say: "One is welcomed everywhere in the world if one is competent technically". After getting an education in the importance of giving prominence to proletarian politics and in correctly handling the relations between politics and technique, the doctor came to realize that a person who masters technique still has to solve the problem of which class he is serving. He said: "I'd gone astray along the bourgeois road of egoism in the past when I gave prominence to technique".

He concluded, "I have made up my mind now to put proletarian politics before everything else and to thoroughly remould my bourgeois world outlook so that I integrate with and serve the workers, peasants and soldiers as long as I live".

Wuhan, Hupeh Provincial Broadcast, 14 June 1969

DOCTORS' ERROR

... Sun Peng-shan, doctor in charge of internal medicine, said: "One night in November last year, a duty doctor reported to me that a patient who had been transferred from the surgery department had suffered a sudden shock. As I began to examine the patient, I recalled that he had twice suffered from bile-duct infection. I made a brief check with my stethoscope, and subjectively decided that this was a recurrence of his old problem. However, other young doctors who had also examined the patient told me that they had heard a murmuring sound in the patient's chest. Yet I summarily dismissed their diagnosis and decided that the patient should undergo an operation.

"Hospital procedures require that major operations

should be reported to the Hospital Revolutionary Committee. In order to solve the controversy in diagnosis, the P.L.A. representative and Chairman of the Revolutionary Committee asked us to check again. Although I too discovered the murmuring after careful examination, I tossed out all sorts of excuses for my subjectivism and egoism to protect my so-called professional dignity.

"I was then rebuked by the others and underwent a fierce ideological struggle. Upon repeated study of Chairman Mao's teaching, I realised that I should struggle against my bourgeois medical ideas and my bourgeois world outlook. I also realized that to become a revolutionary medical worker it is necessary to creatively study and apply the 'three constantly-read articles', establish the proletarian world outlook of serving people 'wholly' and 'thoroughly', and use Mao Tse-tung thought to guide medical practice".

Shen Ho-fei, chief of the internal medicine department, said: "One day in November last year, a pregnant young worker was admitted into the hospital. She was in a deep coma. Her blood pressure was dropping continuously and her condition was critical. On examination, I found that she was suffering from a serious gynaecological disease involving internal haemorrhage, and concluded hat her chances of survival were slim. Although the 30 and more workers who sent her in filled with profound proletarian feeling pleaded with me to save the patient by all means, I still held that her disease was 'incurable'.

"The leading comrade of the Hospital Revolutionary Committee noticed my ideological problem while I was carrying out the examination. He then organized us to study Chairman Mao's teaching: **'this question "for whom" is fundamental; it is a question of principle'**, and set up a rescue team to save the patient.

"As head of a department, I was not at all happy when I was told to observe the treatment as a mere 'special nurse'. Realizing my displeasure, the leading comrade of the Revolutionary Committee immediately helped me study Chairman Mao's work *In memory of Norman*

Bethune, and assigned a Vice-Chairman of the Revolutionary Committee as 'special nurse' to work with me. At that point, I realized that the renegade, hidden traitor and scab Liu Shao-chi's counter-revolutionary revisionist line on medical and health work had coiled round me like a venomous snake. If I did not resolutely and thoroughly transform my bourgeois world outlook, I would not have profound proletarian feelings nor be able to serve the workers, peasants and soldiers whole-heartedly. Then we followed the mass line according to Chairman Mao's teaching and applied the method of combining Western and Chinese medicine, including the use of acupuncture, in our treatment. After much struggle, the patient was saved".

In January this year, the Huakung Hospital in Kirin admitted a child suffering from hydrocephalus, a condition long pronounced by bourgeois specialists and authorities as incurable. However, discarding foreign conventions and following the leadership of the Hospital Revolutionary Committee, the medical workers allowed Mao Tse-tung thought to guide them and, after repeated struggle, they successfully saved the child. The medical workers said: "In the great 1970's we are determined to follow Chairman Mao's teaching and guard against arrogance and rashness. We will persist in carrying out uninterruptedly the struggle-criticism-transformation movement in medical and health work, and do it in a penetrating manner. We will persist in making medical and health work serve the workers, peasants and soldiers, and let Mao Tse-tung thought occupy the medical and health positions".

NCNA, 8 April 1970

Chapter VII

The Frugal, the Pure and the Humble

FRUGAL WEDDINGS

. . . When poor peasant Yin Teh-shan's daughter was about to be married, he said to his wife: "To have a wedding feast runs counter to Mao Tse-tung thought. We must celebrate the wedding in a frugal way". At the time of the wedding, the mother, on behalf of the whole family, presented the daughter with three gifts—a set of *Selected Works of Mao Tse-tung*, a red-tasselled spear and a spade. . .

NCNA, 4 April 1970

*

. . . With the change of family relations, customs have also changed. Young couples no longer give sumptuous feasts or receive gifts of money when they get married. The bridegroom, bride and guests sing revolutionary songs together and study quotations from Chairman Mao's works. Elderly peasants are often invited to tell about their suffering before liberation and to encourage the young people to treasure their present happiness and to follow Chairman Mao in carrying the revolution through to the end . . .

Peking Radio, 14 April 1969

PATIENT GROOM

Wu, currently a member of the standing committee of the Canton Heavy Machiney Plant revolutionary committee, decided to get married in 1966 when he was 31 and his fiancée 26. However, it was just the time when the great proletarian cultural revolution was launched. At the end of 1967 Wu, urged by his parents, was preparing to get married during the Spring Festival; however, the preparatory group for the provincial revolutionary committee was organizing the revolutionary masses to go and learn from Peking, Shanghai, and other places. So his wedding was again postponed. His subsequent plans to get married on 1 May and 1 October 1968 and on 1 January 1969 were also postponed, owing to his participation in the workers' delegation to Peking and in the plant's purification of the class ranks. To date, he is still not married.

In recent years the revolutionary youths have played a fine role in changing the custom, by having a correct approach towards the relationship between revolution and love and marriage in response to the Party's call opposing early marriages and persisting in late marriages . . . All revolutionary youths should dedicate their youth to communism—the most splendid cause of mankind—under the brilliant rays of Mao Tse-tung's thought.

Kanton, Kwangtung Provincial Broadcast, 14 February 1960

NO DOWRY FOR HSUEH-CHIAO

. . . Wang Chu-sheng and his family live in the Tachuan commune in Yiyang County. Wang Hsueh-chiao, his daughter, was soon to be married. What about the bride's dowry? There was a discussion between the father and mother. Wang Chu-sheng is an activist in the living study and application of Mao Tse-tung's thought in his brigade. He would do what Chairman Mao says. The couple studied the teachings of the great leader Chairman Mao: **"The principle of diligence and frugality should be observed in everything"** and we **"must not take a short view and indulge in wastefulness and extravagance"**. Wang Chu-sheng told his wife: "To make a show with a dowry and banquets for a wedding is an old feudal custom, a bourgeois way. We poor and lower-middle peasants should not copy their style. We will act as Chairman Mao teaches". The whole family arrived at a common view by putting Mao Tse-tung's thought in command. They decided to set an example in breaking with old customs and fostering new ones, and practising economy in the wedding. The family decided that there should not be a dowry, as is done in the old way.

According to local custom, when there is a marriage in the neighbourhood or among relatives, people send presents. Supposing relatives and friends came with gifts? Wang Chu-sheng studied Chairman Mao's writings for guidance. Chairman Mao teaches: **"We still have to wage a protracted struggle against bourgeois and petty-bourgeois ideology"**. Wang Chu-sheng thought to himself: "Sending presents is also a feudal, a bourgeois, way of doing things. We poor and lower-middle peasants should pay attention to what Chairman Mao teaches and end these things".

An old friend of Wang Chu-sheng's sent him some money to buy stockings for the bride. Wang Chu-sheng thanked him but would not take the sum. He told the friend: "We appreciate your friendship. But we cannot take your money. We will adhere to Chairman Mao's teachings and break with old customs and habits".

One day, the father of the bridegroom came to visit Wang Chu-sheng. He said: "Your daughter and my son are getting married, and we will be relatives. I'm very sorry I haven't brought you a gift, nor pretty clothes for my new daughter-in-law". Wang Chu-sheng replied: "Both you and I have studied Chairman Mao's works. Let's free ourselves from old customs. If I marry my daughter to your son and you give me gifts, it would be a transaction, wouldn't it? You and I are class brothers, let's smash bourgeois practices". The visitor offered a sum of money for Wang Hsueh-chiao to make some fine clothes. Wang-Chu-sheng earnestly persuaded him not to do it. The bride also said: "I'm used to ordinary clothes for work, not fancy things made of fine fabric". Her future father-in-law was deeply moved and said: "That's right! In arranging the wedding we should follow Chairman Mao's revolutionary line".

On the eve of the wedding, Wang Chu-sheng had many things to tell his daughter before she left his roof. He had in mind this teaching of Chairman Mao: **"Historical experience merits attention. A line or a viewpoint must be explained constantly and repeatedly. It won't do to explain them only to a few people; they must be made known to the broad revolutionary masses".** He wanted to tell his daughter once again about the misery his family had endured in the old society, in order to give her a lesson in class struggle and the history of the struggle between the two lines.

Inviting relatives to his home, Wang Chu-sheng raised his maimed left hand to the lamp and said to his daughter: "You must remember class hatred. In the old society I was an apprentice at the age of 13 in a workshop making steel yards. My boss made money at the expense of the workers' lives. He once handed me a shell and told me to hammer the copper for making steel yards. But there was an explosive charge in the shell, and when I pounded it with a hammer, it exploded.

"When I came to, I found that I was badly hurt. My left hand had been blown off by the explosive. My boss made me leave the hospital before my injuries were healed. Then he drove me out of the workshop.

"It was our great leader Chairman Mao who saved me

from the pit of suffering. With the help of the collective, life has improved day by day for my family. But that rotten Liu Shao-chi preached 'exploitation has its merits' and other trash trying to restore capitalism. Liu Shao-chi is the sworn enemy of us poor and lower-middle peasants. Chairman Mao saved us, and his revolutionary line is our life line. We must always follow Chairman Mao closely, and defend his revolutionary line with our lives".

Wang Hsueh-chiao's father-in-law also told of the harsh life his family had endured when he worked as a farmhand in the old society. He advised the young people always to remember the suffering of their class, never forget class hatred, and always follow Chairman Mao in making revolution.

Wang Hsueh-chiao was an activist in the living study and application of Mao Tse-tung's thought in the production team. She was praised by the commune members as an "iron girl". Wang Chu-sheng thought: "My daughter made progress because the team's poor and lower-middle peasants helped her. If we ask them to give their opinions about her before her marriage, she will make still faster progress with the help of the masses". The team approved of his suggestion. And so there was an unusual party to send off the bride.

Wang Hsueh-chiao eagerly asked the poor and lower-middle peasants to speak freely. They said that she was conscientious in studying Chairman Mao's works and loved collective labour. In addition to her many other good points, they also pointed out her shortcomings and encouraged her to keep up her good record, overcome her shortcomings and make new contributions when she went to her husband's production team.

As his daughter was leaving, Wang Chu-sheng presented her with a set of *Selected Works of Mao Tse-tung*, *Quotations from Chairman Mao Tse-tung*, the "three constantly read articles" of Chairman Mao and two Chairman Mao badges. Holding the treasured revolutionary gifts from her parents, the excited Wang Hsueh-chiao declared that she would always be loyal to

Chairman Mao, to Mao Tse-tung's thought and to Chairman Mao's revolutionary line, and follow Chairman Mao in making revolution all her life.

NCNA, 28 January 1969

NO NEW CLOTHES FOR THE BRIDE

. . . Last year, when I returned to the commune after my participation in the Ninth C.C.P. National Congress, the commune had a new office desk made for me. I refused to accept it because I thought that, although my position had changed, I should not let bourgeois dirt contaminate my thinking.

Chairman Mao teaches us that if the countryside position is not occupied by socialism, it will be occupied by capitalism. A handful of class enemies will invariably try to corrupt the masses with reactionary bourgeois ideas in order to achieve their aim of restoring capitalism. In July of last year, I discovered that a girl who was going to be married asked her fiancé to have some new clothes made for her. Knowing that this was bourgeois thinking, I then organised the poor and lower-middle peasants to attend a forum to study Chairman Mao's teaching **"Never forget class struggle"**.

Peking Radio, 2 May 1970

"SUGAR-COATED BULLETS"

. . . The class enemies may make use of the shortcomings of some comrades who always consider themselves in the right and cannot bear to hear criticism of their work by

118

the masses, and overwhelm them with comfort and consolation . . .

They may resort to such means as indulgence in eating, drinking, and pleasure-seeking, invitations to parties, and presenting gifts and using beautiful women to corrupt the soul. Some of our comrades have thus been dragged into the water in comfort . . .

Wuhan, Hupeh Provincial Broadcast, 16 January 1969

HUMILITY IN OFFICE

. . . Han Yung-Chiu, who works in a post office in Chienhsi County, Hopeh Province, North China, has been praised by the poor and lower-middle peasants as "a good postman serving the people whole-heartedly".

In addition to delivering mail, Han Yung-chiu took on the task of delivering Chairman Mao's works for the bookshop in an effort to propagate Mao Tse-tung thought. During the great proletarian cultural revolution, he has seen to it that Chairman Mao's latest instructions and various proletarian policies get to the broad masses as swiftly as possible. He delivers newspapers to 12 production brigades every day. For this additional work, he has to climb six hills and cover 10 extra kilometres. Carrying his bags weighing some 30 kilogrammes on his back and going from place to place, Han Yung-chiu has never had a word of complaint . . .

Han Yung-chiu was elected to the county revolutionary committee during the great proletarian cultural revolution. Some people said: "Now that you're a member of the county revolutionary committee, how is it you still go into the mountains with your bags?"

He replied: "I've become a member of the revolutionary committee, and this shows that the masses make even higher demands on me. Chairman Mao teaches us: **'Communists seek not official posts, but revolution'**. My position has changed now, but my revolutionary ideology mustn't change. I must always be a revolutionary fighter loyal to Chairman Mao and be a servant of the people all my life".

Peking Radio, 5 June 1969

*

. . . Chiu Chin-mao [vice-chairman of the county revolutionary committee] always joins in manual labour as soon as he returns from a meeting. It was late one evening when the meeting he had attended in the county town was over. He wanted to go back to take part in manual labour the next day. The comrades offered to take him home by car. He refused, saying: "Chairman Mao wore straw sandals when he led the people of the Chingkang Mountains in crossing mountains and rivers to make revolution. Following Chairman Mao, we should travel on foot to break a path and create a Red new world" . . .

NCNA, 10 June 1969

THAUMATURGIC BLACKSMITH

. . . A certain indigenous disease, considered to be incurable by experts and authorities both at home and abroad, has been overcome by comrade Liu Haisochieh, a communist and an ordinary blacksmith of this region. This achievement has filled a big gap in world medicine. This is a handsome gift for the Ninth National C.C.P. Congress from the workers, poor and lower-middle peasants, and people of various nationalities . . .

This innovation in the field of world medicine is a direct blow to the imperialists, revisionists and counter-revolutionaries who have been cursing about our proletarian cultural revolution, as well as a slap in the face for the pseudo-foreign devils, big and small, including Liu Shao-chi. This unprecedented achievement has been brought about by the newborn proletariat and is eloquent testimony of this truth: **"The humble are the most intelligent; the lofty are the most ignorant"**.

"Only heroes can send off the god of plague". Such an event can take place only in an age when workers, peasants and soldiers can master Marxism-Leninism and Mao Tse-tung's thought. The reason why the humble are the most intelligent is that they have the warmest love for and loyalty to the invincible thought of Mao Tse-tung. Once they master Mao Tse-tung's thought, a powerful ideological weapon, they have the courage to think, act and break through; they have the courage to look down on all reactionary authorities and cast to the winds the slavish philosophy of admiring foreign devils and abiding by foreign rules and regulations. Devotion to public interest begets political consciousness, wisdom and strength. While scaling the pinnacle of world science, they destroy all resistance in their way.

Whenever they lack material, they make their own discovery; whenever they lack medical supplies, they manufacture them; whenever they lack the know-how, they think it out. No problems, however long-standing, big, or difficult, can intimidate them. With Mao Tse-tung's thought, they can transform consciousness into material force and perform any miracle . . .

Huhehot, Inner Mongolian Regional Broadcast, 18 March 1969

EXALTING THE LOWLY

. . . Trial manufacture began in the factory in October 1966. Harbouring inveterate hatred for this new born thing, the handful of capitalist roaders in the Party and the class enemies in the factory did everything they could to obstruct and sabotage the undertaking. They slandered the revolutionary workers, saying, "scientific experiments are the affair of technicians and university graduates. How can you workers expect to produce any bacteria? You don't know how high the sky is and how big the earth is!"

The revolutionary workers replied firmly in words like these: "Chairman Mao says: **'The humble are the most intelligent; the lofty are the most ignorant'**. Armed with Mao Tse-tung's thought, the working class is capable of performing worders which you cannot even imagine!" They chose four comrades with only primary school education to study for one month at a unit which was then carrying out experiments in making the new insecticide. After the four comrades, returned the workers borrowed a microscope, bought several flasks, made some wooden cases and immediately started their experiments . . .

Devoted to serving the people **"wholly"** and **"entirely"**, they went to the villages to make investigations and canvass the poor and lower-middle peasants for their views. In doing this, they made more and more progress in their experiments. Over 900 experiments in all were conducted and they finally succeeded in trial producing the new type of insecticide.

Peking Radio, 15 March 1969

"THANK CHAIRMAN MAO"

. . . A lower-middle peasant, Hu Chia-pao, who had an abscess on his foot, had been treated in a hospital for over 40 days without being cured. By the time someone brought him to Liao Shih-ching [a Hunan barefoot doctor] the abscess had already so festered that there was a cavity in one piece of bone and pus flowed in several places. Hu Chia-pao was most pessimistic about his condition.

The first thing Liao Shih-ching did was to study with him this great teaching of Chairman Mao: **"In times of difficulty we must not lose sight of our achievements, must see the bright future and must pluck up our courage"** to strengthen his belief that the disease could be conquered. Together, they afterwards studied other articles by Chairman Mao.

When Hu Chia-pao had completely recovered and returned home, he sent Liao some gifts to express his gratitude. Liao thought: "As a servant of the people, I should not accept gifts the way the lordly doctors in the old society used to do. This shows that Hu Chia-pao still has the old idea of giving a reward to someone who has helped him. I must help him change his old ideas".

Instead of accepting his gifts, Liao bought two sets of the *Selected Works of Mao Tse-tung*, five copies of Chairman Mao's five constantly read articles, and portraits of Chairman Mao and sent them to Hu Chia-pao and his production team. He said to Hu: "You need not thank me. You should thank our great leader Chairman Mao. There would be no Liao Shih-ching today but for Chairman Mao. And if I were not armed with Mao Tse-tung thought, I couldn't have cured you either".

In the last three years or so, Liao Shih-ching has given 14,000 treatments, cured 156 dangerous and emergency cases, including cases that had been treated by big hospitals without result, and by famous doctors who could not help.

Peking Radio, 31 May 1969

ASCETIC STOREKEEPER

. . . For the past 18 years, Ma Hsing-li has thoughtfully handled money and material for socialism, and people call him a socialist "Red housekeeper" for his public-spiritedness. Over the past 18 years, he has never taken a Sunday off. During the climax of struggle-criticism-transformation in the store in 1968, he even stayed in the store for five months without going home in order to have more time for revolutionary work. For the past 18 years of working in stores he has never taken a single penny from the State.

For the past 10 years or more, Ma Hsing-li has also maintained, in accordance with Chairman Mao's teaching, the style of arduous struggle and plain living. When he was transferred to the Kaoyi store as manager in 1962, he did all the manual labour—cleaning floors, hauling vegetables and selling things. He even picked up tins discarded as refuse. Under the leadership and influence of Ma Hsing-li, it has become a habit for the store workers to work hard and practise economy.

Although the party organisation has asked Ma Hsing-li to move to a new house from the cow shed of a rich man, where he has lived for more than 20 years, he has refused, saying: "Staying in this house always reminds me of class suffering and that there are many labouring people who are still suffering in the world. Keeping this in mind makes one more vigorous in making revolution".

NCNA, 7 April 1970

COW-DUNG CURES IDEOLOGICAL DISEASE

. . . For Wang Yung-yi, a doctor educated in a medical college, this was the first time he had gone to the countryside. He lived with an old cattle-tender called

Uncle Chu. At first, he couldn't stand the smell of the cow-dung and the dirt around where they slept. And when the old man got up to feed the animals in the middle of the night, it greatly annoyed him. So Uncle Chu got him to study the three constantly read articles and check his thinking in the light of Chairman Mao's teachings. Seeing that the old man took better care of the collective cattle than himself and that he got up at night every day to tend the animals, Wang Yung-yi was deeply moved by the old man's noble quality of utter devotion to the collective. From the old man he saw how removed he himself was from the poor and lower-middle peasants in class spirit and feeling. He made up his mind to make up the distance by physical labour. During the day he treated the poor and lower-middle peasants, helped Uncle Chu prepare the fodder and tidy up the cattle shed and also took part in other farm work. At night he got up to feed the cattle for Uncle Chu. Wang Yung-yi said: "The smell of cow-dung doesn't matter, but if my thinking stinks, it matters a lot. Only when I am helped by the poor and lower-middle peasants to cure my ideological disease, can I serve them whole-heartedly and cure their diseases" . . .

Peking Radio, 2 August 1969

Chapter VIII

Spreading the Word

RED BARDS

... "I had the honour to become a revolutionary story-teller back in late December of 1962, a few months after Chairman Mao called on us never to forget class struggle. Inspired by the solicitude and teachings of Chairman Mao, and with the support of the leadership at all levels and the broad revolutionary masses who have persisted in the proletarian revolutionary line, I told revolutionary stories on some 820 occasions within a few months to a total of more than 180,000 people. I have told 60 different revolutionary stories, including 'Rent Collection Courtyard', 'Lei Feng', 'Chang Ssu-te', 'The Red Lantern', 'Norman Bethune', 'Chiao Yu-lu', 'Tsai Yung-hsiang', 'Thoroughly Overthrow Liu Shao-chi' ...

"Besides telling stories in my county, I have also travel-led to Chuansha, Manhui, Shanghai and Chinshan counties to tell stories in universities, middle and elementary schools, in the fields and neighbourhoods, on project sites, and in railway stations, teahouses, offices, factories and other public places.

"My past experience in telling revolutionary stories has strengthened my belief that the propagation of Mao Tse-tung thought is my fundamental task. I will be a revolutionary storyteller and fight on the rural ideo-logical front for the rest of my life".

Hsu Chu-chen and Hsu Min-na, storytellers from Chingpu County, said: "In 1962, the capitalist forces launched a frantic offensive against our party, and many demons and monsters stepped out one after another. The tea houses became places for them to praise the emperors and kings, generals and ministers and scholars and beauties.

"Under this new situation of class struggle, which was as acute as it was complicated, the party instructed us to use literary and art propaganda methods as weapons to seize the cultural fronts and to propagate Mao Tse-tung thought extensively. Inspired by the active advocation and the enthusiastic support of the late Comrade Ko Ching-shih, a good student of Chairman Mao, we of the story section made it a practice vigorously to tell revolutionary stories to the broad revolutionary masses on Sundays and holidays. We told revolutionary stories in the streets, the countryside, the teahouses, the railway stations, on the docks and in hospital wards" . . .

Ou [a storyteller of the Kunghui commune] asked: "Where do we find material for our stories? Do we ask others or do we rely on ourselves?"

He said: "Adhering to Chairman Mao's great call to rely on our own efforts, we have sought to compile revolutionary stories from local materials. Under the leadership and solicitude of the Party, our brigade organized a contingent of storywriters, made up of poor and lower-middle peasants, educated youths, and educated youths who had settled in the countryside as the main components. The party branch in the brigade attaches great importance to the political and ideological education of this contingent of storywriters. Periodic Mao Tse-tung thought study classes have been run for the revolutionary storytellers and the storywriters. They are also invited to attend various important meetings held in the brigade.

"The materials for our stories are adapted from speeches made by the peasants in the mass criticism and repudiation meetings, or from the advanced deeds of peasants in production. In the past years, our brigade has created more than 60 revolutionary stories based on our ardent love for Chairman Mao, Mao Tse-tung thought, and Chairman Mao's revolutionary line, as well as our hatred for Liu Shao-chi. We have compiled stories to repudiate all the fallacies of Liu Shao-chi, with a story for each one of his fallacies" . . .

Shanghai Radio, 24 June 1969

SINGING TO A PURPOSE

A number of historical revolutionary songs, familiar to many comrades during the period of the anti-Japanese and liberation wars, have had their words changed by the collective efforts of the revolutionary literature and art workers. The leadership of Chairman Mao and the C.C.P., and the great ideology of Chairman Mao regarding the people's army and people's war and the revolutionary role of the workers, peasants and the masses have all been stressed. They have been warmly welcomed by the masses of workers, peasants and soldiers throughout the nation.

Particularly at a time when the great leader Chairman Mao has made a solemn statement in support of the struggle of the world's people against US imperialism, the singing of historical revolutionary songs can further arouse the workers, peasants and soldiers and the masses, foster the revolutionary spirit and encourage the will to struggle, to pursue to the end the revolution in China and in the world, along the paths of proletarian revolutionary struggle solemnly pointed out by Chairman Mao.

Factories, farms, offices and schools in various localities should all treat the task of teaching and singing historical revolutionary songs as an important element in political and class education. It should be grasped as a political task. A campaign to learn and sing revolutionary songs should be launched rapidly.

Wuhan, Hupeh Provincial Broadcast, 24 May 1970

LITTLE RED SOLDIERS

. . . Over the four years since the little red soldiers were organized, they have persisted in studying Chairman Mao's works. Nine-year-old Tsai Mei-jung does not know many characters but she is unafraid of difficulties. She often carries *Quotations from Chairman Mao Tse-tung* and the "three constantly read articles" with her. She studies while tending the ox or in the fields. Sometimes, before going to bed, she recites the "three constantly read articles". Now she is letter-perfect in reciting the "three constantly read articles" and more than 100 quo tations from Chairman Mao. Of more than 80 little red soldiers in the village, more than half can recite the "three constantly read articles" and dozens of quotations from Chairman Mao.

The little red soldiers have organized a Mao Tse-tung thought propaganda team, which often helps women and old people study Chairman Mao's works and his latest instructions. Some of these adults are illiterate, so the little red soldiers teach them sentence by sentence. During busy farm seasons, the little red soldiers go to the fields to spread Mao Tse-tung thought through performances. Whenever new instructions of Chairman Mao's are published, the little red soldiers on duty immediately notify all the members and spread them to every poor and lower-middle peasant family . . .

NCNA, 31 May 1969

*

. . . These little red soldiers are also constantly launching offensives against the class enemies. They have turned their station into "a powerful weapon to unite and educate the people, and attack and annihilate the enemies".

There was a reactionary rich peasant in the Chiaotzukou brigade who frequently stole collective property and undermined the collective economy. The little red soldiers felt this was an attempt by the class enemies to undermine socialism. It was therefore a class struggle. They immediately collected material about the crimes of this rich peasant in undermining the collective economy, and broadcast them for several nights. Unable to bear this, the villain sneaked away to Hsienchingkou, two li away. The little red soldiers gave chase to him right on his heels by climbing over the hills. When they arrived at Hsienchingkou, they continued to broadcast the villain's crimes. Thus, the villain was so repudiated that he could find no place to hide.

With the help of the revolutionary teachers, the little red soldiers realized that one must be red ideologically before one can propagate Mao Tse-tung thought. In their work, they have always given first importance to studying Chairman Mao's works, following his teachings and working in accordance with his instructions, so as to revolutionize their own thinking.

Apart from Chairman Mao's works, which they learn in class, they also make it a practice to run Mao Tse-tung thought study classes to combine study with their own thinking, and to fight self-interest and repudiate revisionism in order to establish the ideology of complete and thorough service to the people. During the spring of 1969, they made a suggestion to all production brigades in the commune that the little red soldiers' radio station be run in a big way. Their suggestion immediately received the support of the commune revolutionary committee. In a matter of a few days, each brigade had set up such a station. Impressed by these new stations, many brigades in the other communes of the county also set up their own little red soldiers' radio stations. This brigade's poor and lower-middle peasants have composed a song of praise, which says:
> The little red soldiers broadcasting station,
> Carries out propaganda in spite of wind or snow,
> Latest instructions are delivered to the doorsteps,
> What worthy successors these little red soldiers are!

Peking Radio, 30 May 1969

TREE-TOP BROADCASTERS

A "red youth broadcasting team" disseminating Mao Tse-tung thought has been in operation since 1964 at the Houwuwang production brigade under Paitaokou commune in Hua County, Honan.

At the end of each day members of the team climb up trees and onto housetops to spread Chairman Mao's words with their megaphones. They have been doing their job so well that the poor and lower-middle peasants of the brigade hail them as "the red youth megaphone team".

Born out of the mass movement of creatively studying and applying Mao Tse-tung thought initiated in 1964, the red youth megaphone team of the Houwuwang production brigade has grown and been tempered in the great proletarian cultural revolution. The team now consists of more than 110 children, ranging in age from six to 15.

During the period of the Ninth National C.C.P. Congress, members of the team used their megaphones to broadcast the communiqués of the Congress three times a day among the peasants. On one of those days it was especially cold, but the children of the red youth megaphone team braved the bitter winds to disseminate Chairman Mao's latest instructions everywhere around the commune. Commune members said: "With their hearts turning toward Chairman Mao, these children are worthy to be called red youths of the Mao Tse-tung era".

Fearing that the peasants might not have clearly heard Chairman Mao's latest instructions through their megaphone broadcasting, four members of the team toured the commune at midnight and wrote Chairman Mao's instructions on the "Quotations from Chairman Mao" board hung on the door of every peasant household. It was morning by the time they completed the tour.

NCNA, 31 May 1969

EVERY HOME SHOULD HAVE ONE

. . . As the mass movement of struggle-criticism-transformation progresses, the poor and lower-middle peasants and commune members of Kuanshe brigade are also implementing the creative study and application of Mao Tse-tung's thought on an individual household basis. However, some households have fallen behind in this effort to revolutionize ideology. The party branch at the brigade found many reasons for this, the main one being that the heads of these households themselves were all lagging behind other household heads in the creative study and application of Mao Tse-tung's thought.

The party branch at the brigade realized that, in order to ensure that each household succeeds in the creative study and application of Mao Tse-tung's thought and in ideological revolutionization, the remaining influence of the feudal system of respecting the leadership of the head of the household must be eradicated, and the leader of the household must be the one who is doing best in the creative study and application of Mao Tse-tung's thought. After consulting with the peasants, a system of establishing a political instructor in each household was set up. Under this system, the members of each household evaluate and elect one of their own numbers to be the instructor.

The evaluation and election of a household political instructor involves an acute political revolution in the household. In one household the grandmother wanted to elect her daughter-in-law, but her grandson thought his father should be elected. The father had been seriously afflicted with the feudalistic notion of the authority of the husband, and voted for himself. His wife dared not speak up, and the man was elected. When this was brought out at a meeting of the peasants of the brigade, all present voted for the wife and she was elected.

At first, the man could not swallow his defeat. But his wife told him: "The great proletarian cultural revolution is aimed at destroying the old and establishing the new. We must follow those whose opinion conforms with Mao Tse-tung's thought". With her help, the husband finally examined his incorrect attitude in front of the other peasants, saying:

"In the past I did not apply well what I had studied of Chairman Mao's works. My wife is not educated but she was able to apply what little she had learned. She certainly is better than I and should be the household political instructor".

Now the household political instructors are daily leading members of their own households in studying Chairman Mao's works, and Chairman Mao's latest instructions are conveyed in the household study classes. The political instructors are also leading their household members to carry out mass repudiation of the revisionist fallacies pushed by Liu Shao-chi. The instructors themselves are also attending study classes run for them by the party branch to help them bring their role as political instructors into full play in the households.

NCNA, 1 April 1969

"WHOLE FAMILY RED"

... Now there are lecture cells in the families and lecture teams in the production teams, lecture sub-groups in the production brigades, and a lecture group in the commune. There are 110 lecture contingents with more than 1,800 members. These comrades who lecture are very active. There are teams of grandfathers and grandsons, mothers-in-law and daughters-in-law, brothers, sisters, and husbands and wives. There are also teams of 'Whole Families Red', 'Three Red Generations', 'Five Old Men', and 'Eight Old Nannies'. At first, they lectured with the help of 'the five constantly read articles', *On Contradiction*, and *On Practice* have been used.

The "Whole Family Red" movement has greatly promoted the creative study and application of Mao Tse-tung thought among the peasants. Everywhere and at every moment they are seen studying together, criticizing revisionism, fighting self-interest, and discussing state affairs together. Now the commune has 653 activists in the creative study and application of Mao Tse-tung thought, 2,030 instructors in Chairman Mao's works, 1,222 household Mao Tse-tung thought study classes and 778 combined-household study classes which link the nearly 3,000 peasant households of the commune.

As the movement develops, many five-good commune members have emerged. The old relationship among members of a family has changed into one of revolutionary comradeship. While in the past discussions in a family centered on family affairs, love, and personal gain, the conversations now turn to Mao Tse-tung thought, good people and deeds, and farming for the revolution – a peasant has sacrificed his life in rescuing others, while another has exposed the crime of her father-in-law in covering up a counter-revolutionary . . .

Nanchang, Kiangsi Provincial Broadcast, 26 September 1969

STREET STUDY

. . . Since March 1968, some 200 Mao-thought study courses have been held, with attendances totalling over 90 per cent of the residents. The brilliance of Mao Tse-tung's thought has shone in all households, eliminating all dirt still remaining in the gloomy corners of the street. The mental outlook of residents has undergone profound change. Many have shown keen interest in state affairs and the proletarian dictatorship, breaking away from the confinement of the home. The residents have spontaneously launched revolutionary great repudiation, and resolutely smashed the rightist reversal of verdicts, counter-revolutionary economism, and speculation and profiteering launched by the class enemies. They have reformed the leaders of two gangs of hooligans and thieves and a number of bad elements.

. . . The personnel of the Huangtuling hero company guided the members of the Mao-study courses to concentrate their hatred on the class enemies. An old woman, who had been afraid to expose the sabotage activities of bad elements, became bold enough to struggle against the class enemies after studying the "three constantly read articles". She exposed a bad man in the act of perpertrating a crime. Another woman informed on three bad elements.

The Mao-thought study courses conducted by the hero company took a variety of forms in the light of the characteristics of the street, giving every resident a chance to take part in study. The P.L.A. personnel encouraged the basic-level cadres, instructors, primary school children and little red soldiers to give full play to their activism. They also took into consideration the actual difficulties of housewives and old people. A paralyzed woman with a sick father was helped by the little red soldiers and her neighbours at the request of the P.L.A. She was so grateful that Chairman Mao had saved her that she crawled with the help of two stools to attend the study course. The No. 8 residents' committee always had greater attendances than expected in its five Mao-study courses. Some old men continued to study in one course after another and would not leave. Enthusiasm for study was universally high.

Canton, Kwantung Provincial Broadcast, 7 June 1968

TRAINING

. . . Every day many railway trains leave and arrive in Peking to and from all parts of China. These trains have been turned into great red schools of Mao Tse-tung's thought. The railway workers and staff members in Peking live nearest to Chairman Mao, follow him most closely, and are most loyal to him. They consider the spreading of Mao Tse-tung's thought their most glorious task and most sacred duty. Every time one of Chairman Mao's instructions is published, they immediately bring it to the attention of the passengers, study it, and hold celebrations on board the trains.

They have overcome many difficulties and insisted on holding Mao Tse-tung's thought study classes on board the trains, in order to organize the masses of passengers to study Mao Tse-tung's thought. In the study classes, special attention is paid to the good revolutionary style of study – linking theory and practice – and it is stressed that one should apply what one has studied. The people's trains have become battlefields for repudiating Liu Shao-chi's sinister book on self-cultivation. The trains have become positions from which to strike down the big renegade Liu Shao-chi. The Peking railway workers constantly hold revolutionary mass repudiation sessions on the trains vigorously to expose and repudiate the towering crimes of the big renegade Liu Shao-chi and to praise the great wisdom of the great leader Chairman Mao.

In the great proletarian cultural revolution, the great Chinese People's Liberation Army has sent its most outstanding fighters to serve on the people's trains. The fighters enthusiastically spread Mao Tse-tung's thought and wholeheartedly serve the masses of passengers. At the same time, they maintain high vigilance against sabotage and trouble making by the handful of class enemies, and heroically protect the safety of the people's trains . . .

Peking Radio, 27 February 1969

AIRBORNE WITH CHAIRMAN MAO

Air hostess Tsao Chun-ling has overcome selfish ideas and now propagates Mao's thoughts in an exemplary manner. During a flight from Lanchow to Peking, she greeted the passengers by leading them in cheering "A long, long life to Chairman Mao" and then held a combat-self-interest-and-repudiate-revisionism session which lasted for most of the flight. When she was called upon to turn the aircraft into a position for the dissemination of Mao's thought, she worried that her educational, theoretical and political level was not high enough. However, aided by a study of the relevant quotations from Chairman Mao, she learned to dance, recite poems and ballads and sing Peking and Yuehchu Opera and to use them as instruments for the propagation of Chairman Mao's thought.

NCNA, 17 November 1967

Chapter IX

Loving Chairman Mao

CHAIRMAN MAO IN HIS BODILY REALITY

. . . A thunderous ovation resounded through the Great Hall of the People. Excited faces turned to Chairman Mao like sunflowers to the sun. With overflowing enthusiasm and happiness, the revolutionary fighters waved their copies of *Quotations from Chairman Mao Tse-tung* and, with great feeling, continuously shouted: "Long live Chairman Mao!", "Long live the victory of the great proletarian cultural revolution!", "Long live the victory of Chairman Mao's revolutionary line!", "Long live the great thought of Mao Tse-tung!" and "Long live Chairman Mao, a long, long life to him!" . . .

After the reception, the revolutionary fighters joyfully sang, "The heavens are great, the earth is great, but they can't compare with the greatness of what the Party has done for the people. Dear as are father and mother, Chairman Mao is dearer" . . .

Many wrote on the flyleaf of their treasured red books: "At 7.30 p.m., 14 November 1967, I met Chairman Mao, the red sun that shines most brightly in our hearts".

NCNA, 14 November, 1967

*

"When you beamingly, radiantly, and walking with steady stride, waved at us, fighters from the four seas immediately jumped for joy with warm tears in their eyes. Like spring wind, the great news blew 10,000 li to the seas and rivers. Mountains heartily cheered and the vast seas sang lustily. Our supreme commander is in such good mental and physical health! This is the greatest happiness for people throughout the whole world, as well as for the Chinese people. All of us naval commanders and fighters repeatedly cheered you: 'Long life, long life, long, long life' and time and again wished you, 'long life, long life, and long life'.

"All rivers flow into the sea and every Red heart turns toward the sun. Oh Chairman Mao, Chairman Mao, the mountains are tall, but not as tall as the blue sky. Rivers are deep, but not as deep as the ocean. Lamps are bright, but not as bright as the sun and moon. Your kindness is taller than the sky, deeper than the ocean, and brighter than the sun and moon. It is possible to count the stars in the highest heavens, but it is impossible to count your contributions to mankind" . . .

Peking Radio, 6 December 1967

*

The Tibetian woman, Pasang, turned to Chairman Mao, extended both hands to him and as he shook hands said: "I felt a warm invigorating current pass through me. Dearest Chairman Mao, with this pair of hands of yours you have steered the Chinese revolution steadily forward through all tempests and storms, bypassed the submerged rocks and broken through the dark tunnel of night to lead us from victory to victory. It is with this pair of hands that you have written treasured revolutionary works and guided the labouring people of the whole country in revolution and socialist construction. And with this pair of hands you have indicated to all the oppressed peoples of the world the bright road to winning freedom and independence".

NCNA, 25 November 1966

*

"Our dearest, great leader Chairman Mao: You personally approved the invitation to us by the Party's Central Committee, with you as its leader and Vice Chairman

Lin as its deputy leader, to attend National Day celebrations. During this important festivity, we were
fortunate in seeing you. At 17 minutes past six o'clock
this afternoon, you again received us at the Great Hall
of the People. This was a moment we shall never forget.
We saw you walk with firm steps, smile, and wave your
hands toward us. We were all overjoyed. Your radiant
face, excellent health, and vigorous spirit provide the
greatest happiness for the people of China and revolutionary people throughout the world.

"Chairman Mao! We had thought of you every day
and night. Now we have finally seen you".

Nanking, Kiangsu Provincial Broadcast, 12 October 1969

PAINTING THE "RED SUN IN OUR HEARTS"

The Red Guard who did the oil painting "Chairman
Mao Goes to Anyuan" has described how it was painted
in an article in *People's Daily*: "Singing the praises of our
great leader Chairman Mao is our greatest happiness".

The painting was collectively designed by a group of
Peking university and college students. Liu Chun-hua,
a 24-year-old student of the Central Institute of Arts and
Crafts, did the actual painting. This is regarded as the
first revolutionary oil painting illustrating the true
history of Chairman Mao's leadership of the Chinese
workers' movement and shows him in his 20s. A summary
of Lui Chun-hua's article follows:

"What workers, peasants, soldiers and Red Guards
in their hundreds of millions keenly want is for brushes
and paint to be used to portray the noble image of our
great leader Chairman Mao, and paintings be used to
disseminate Mao Tse-tung's thought and sing the praises
of Chairman Mao's revolutionary line. We revolutionary
artists regard this as our fundamental and most glorious
task.

"Chairman Mao received Red Guards on many occasions during the unprecedented great proletarian cultural revolution. The sight of his tall figure and kindly face, and of him smiling and waving his hand to us, thrilled me. I shouted at the top of my voice: 'Long live Chairman Mao! A long, long life to him!' On those occasions I had a great desire to paint a picture of him. The handful of counter revolutionary revisionists used various pretexts in the past to prevent us from singing the praises of Chairman Mao. Now we wield our brushes to extol our great leader, the Red sun shining in our hearts . . .

"We visited the Anyuan coal mine where Chairman Mao lit the flames of revolution. The most essential thing in creating the painting was to present the brilliant image and great thought of our great leader Chairman Mao during his youth. We had an extensive collection of articles and poems written by Chairman Mao in his youth, reminiscences of his revolutionary activities and historical data about Anyuan. We placed Chairman Mao in the forefront of the painting, advancing toward us like a rising sun bringing hope to the people.

"Through meaningful details, we tried to bring out the significance of Chairman Mao's action: his head held high in the act of surveying the scene before him conveys his revolutionary spirit, dauntless before danger and violence, courageous in struggle, and daring to win. His clenched fist depicts his revolutionary will, fearless of all sacrifice and determined to surmount every difficulty to emancipate China and mankind, and shows his confidence in victory. The old umbrella under his right arm shows his hardworking style of travelling in all weather over great distances, across mountains and rivers, for the revolutionary cause. Striding firmly over rugged terrain, Chairman Mao is seen blazing the trail for us, breaking through obstacles in the way of our advance and leading us forward to victory. The hair grown long in a very busy life is blown by the autumn wind. His long plain gown, fluttering in the wind, is a harbinger of the approaching revolutionary storm. The sun is rising, touching the Anyuan hills with red. With the arrival of our great leader, blue skies appear over Anyuan. The hills, sky, trees and clouds are means used to evoke artistically the great image of the Red sun in our hearts.

"The clouds are depicted as Chairman Mao describes in a poem—"Riotous clouds drift past, swift and tranquil". They indicate that Chairman Mao is arriving in Anyuan at a moment of sharp class struggle and show in contrast how tranquil, confident and firm Chairman Mao is at that moment. They also portend the new storm of class struggle that will soon begin.

"In creating this work we felt that the portrayal of Chairman Mao's facial expression was the most difficult and essential thing. The key to solving this problem is to grasp Mao Tse-tung's thought and use it as a guide. We became convinced that we should strive for an expression of revolutionary farsightedness and heroism of Chairman Mao. We should show Chairman Mao's great determination to wholeheartedly serve the emancipation of China and mankind and reflect his unswerving revolutionary spirit, fearing neither danger nor obstacles. In short, we should show that the Red sun in our hearts is the most talented, outstanding and brilliant leader among those who emerge only once in hundreds of years in the history of the world and once in several thousand years in China.

"We collected and studied the few available photographs taken of Chairman Mao in his youth and made repeated sketches and studies from them. In this way we did our best to capture his physical appearance and spirit at that period. We also collected and studied photographs taken at later periods, including those taken during the great proletarian cultural revolution. We blended all we had seen and thought to evolve an image of our great leader Chairman Mao in his youth.

"In our mind's eye we seemed to see the Anyuan miners in the '20s under the threefold oppression of imperialism, feudalism and bureaucratic capitalism in an abyss of suffering, filled with wrath, and longing for the early arrival of the great leader.

"A Red sun suddenly broke through the dark clouds over the Anyuan hills. We saw Chairman Mao walking toward Anyuan. We were very excited and felt we must present all this through the medium of our painting.

"We put aside all the photographs of Chairman Mao and tried to paint the Red sun in our hearts as we felt the scene. Again and again I painted it and solicited opinions from old workers and other comrades as I worked. I wanted to reflect the finest impressions that the revolutionary people have of Chairman Mao. I painted day and night. In the grip of creation, I often forgot to eat. I wanted to impress our deep feelings on canvas. As Chairman Mao's image took shape before me, my will to paint grew.

"Chairman Mao crossed hills and rivers to visit Anyuan on many occasions between 1921 and 1930 to lead the workers in waging revolutionary struggles. It is Chairman Mao who lit the spark of revolution in Anyuan. It is Chairman Mao who made the wise decision to launch a big strike in Anyuan and called on the workers to struggle resolutely. It is Chairman Mao who planned in Anyuan the autumn harvest uprising which shook the world, built the first workers' and peasants' army, and led it to the Chingkang Mountains, thus opening up the road for encirclement of the cities from the countryside and of the seizure of political power by armed force. The great revolutionary practice of Chairman Mao in Anyuan is an epic of unmatched heroism and grandeur. We look on it as a glory and joy to be able to depict an incident from it.

"Over a long period China's Khrushchev described the Anyuan workers' struggle that Chairman Mao led as his contribution. In order to realize his aim of usurping party and state power, he made arrangements for the production of expensive paintings and films and fabricated reminiscences to portray him, a scab and a clown.

as 'the hero who led the Anyuan workers in struggle'. We, the Red Guards of Chairman Mao, must set right the history that was distorted by China's Khrushchev!

"Chairman Mao teaches that our purpose is **'to ensure that literature and art fit well into the whole revolutionary machine as a component part, that they operate as powerful weapons for uniting and educating the people and for attacking and destroying the enemy'**. With boundless love for Chairman Mao and burning hatred for China's Khrushchev, we did this oil painting. We felt we were not just wielding our brushes but were fighting in defence of Chairman Mao and his revolutionary line" . . .

Peking Radio, 9 July 1968

THE POWER OF CHAIRMAN MAO'S IMAGE

. . . Mai Hsien-teh was unconscious or semi-conscious for quite a long time after being admitted to hospital. People anxiously awaited his regaining consciousness, the nurse tested his reactions by showing him a pictorial magazine. As she turned over the pages she noticed his lips quivering. His eyes were concentrated on a picture of Chairman Mao. With great effort he managed to raise his left hand, which had remained useless since his admission to hospital, and with trembling fingers he touched the picture . . .

He suddenly exclaimed "Chairman Mao!" It was the first time since he had been in hospital that he had spoken so clearly.

The image of the great Chairman Mao and his brilliant thought roused Mai Hsien-teh from his stupor. He became fully conscious and was able to think clearly.

He had forgotten nearly everything that had happened previously, but thoughts of the great leader

Chairman Mao were so deeply engraved on his mind that even when only semi-conscious he immediately answered clearly "Chairman Mao" when asked who is the great leader of all the nationalities in China . . .

Peking Review, No. 51, 15 December 1967

*

After the great cultural revolution had begun, every time [Men Ho] came home from his army unit, the first thing he did was to polish the glass of the frame on Chairman Mao's portrait until it glittered. Every morning after getting up, he led his children in singing *The East Is Red* before the portrait of Chairman Mao. He often got the whole family together to study quotations from Chairman Mao. He taught his children to recognize Chairman Mao's portrait and to cheer "Long live Chairman Mao!" even before they learnt to say "papa" and "mama". Once, as he hugged little five-year-old Ching-tsang he pointed to a portrait of Chairman Mao and said: "Child! Chairman Mao is dearer to you than your father and mother. He is the dearest of all in our family. You should always keep Chairman Mao in mind!" Another time, he came back home with 12 portraits of Chairman Mao; he unframed his own picture and those of the children and put Chairman Mao's portrait in their place. Holding up the frame with Chairman Mao's portrait in it, he gazed at it with increasing feeling. Then he said with elation: "This is excellent. Every time we look up, we'll see Chairman Mao. This will give us inexhaustible drive in making revolution!" . . .

Peking Review, No. 24, 14 June 1968

*

Every morning, holding copies of *Quotations from Chairman Mao Tse-tung*, the fighters solemnly pledge to their great leader that they will study his writings, follow his teachings and act according to his instructions all their lives. They pledge that they will defend Chairman Mao, the thought of Mao Tse-tung and his proletarian revolutionary line even at the cost of their lives and be red soldiers loyal to the Party, the people and Chairman Mao. Then they begin the day's activities. Every evening, the pairs of soldiers sit in front of a portrait of Chairman Mao and examine what they have thought and done during the day in the light of Mao Tse-tung's thought.

Red Flag, 24 November 1967

*

... With boundless respect and boundless concern for the great leader Chairman Mao, they gathered around their radio sets and the loudspeakers installed in their villages to listen [to Mao's speech] from beginning to end. While listening it seemed as if they saw with their own eyes our most, most respected great Chairman Mao standing in radiance on the Tien An Men rostrum; they could feel the boundless closeness and happiness in their hearts.

Sian Radio, 8 December 1966 *reporting the reaction of the people of Yenan on the 20th anniversary of the New China Broadcasting Station.*

*

... "With Chairman Mao's portrait hung in the warship, our way will not be lost despite giant waves; with Chairman Mao's portrait hung in the submarine, a ray of sun shines under the sea; with Chairman Mao's portrait hung in the aircraft, the cockpit is brighter than outside; with Chairman Mao's portrait in the combat post, our hearts are red, vision clear, and fighting spirit high; with Chairman Mao's portrait hung on the battlefield, it is like standing guard in Tien An Men Square".

Peking Radio, 6 December 1967

*

. . . While fighting a fire on 16 August, the commanders and fighters of the Mao Tse-tung's thought propaganda team, demonstrating their revolutionary spirit of boundless love for and infinite loyalty to the great leader Chairman Mao, the Party and the people, first braved heavy smoke and raging fire to save from the conflagration Chairman Mao's portrait and a quotation-poster on the wall. And then, with most profound class feeling and noblest spirit of self-sacrifice, fighting together with the masses, moved out a large quantity of food grain. Disregarding their own safety the commanders and fighters of the propaganda team also rescued six revolutionary people and young Red Guard fighters . . .

Heilungkiang Provincial Broadcast, 13 December 1967

*

. . . One poor old peasant called Aunt Sung, who lived in misery in the old society for most of her life, was stricken with cancer of the pancreas . . .

She got worse. She could neither eat, nor sleep, but she asked her daughters to read quotations from Chairman Mao's works and the "three constantly read articles" to her every day. One day, Aunt Sung knew that she was past all help and called her daughters to her bedside, asking the eldest to bring the portrait of Chairman Mao over to her. She looked hard at it for a long time and, her eyes full of tears, said to them: "Girls, now Mao Tse-tung's thought is the guide for our family and my heart is at ease. You must bear in mind that although your parents are dear, they are not

147

as dear to you as Chairman Mao. You must follow him in the revolution all your lives" . . .

Peking Radio, 30 March 1969

*

. . . When he looked up at Chairman Mao's portrait on the wall, he called to mind Chairman Mao's teachings on daring to fight and fearing no difficulties and became even more determined. Though he had never heard of such a disease, he recalled his experience in curing paralysis and inserted a needle into Chang Li-chung's right leg three times.

Immediately, the patient could move his leg. With added confidence, Chen inserted the needle three times into Chang's left leg. He then told the patient: "Old Chang! Try to stand up and take a few steps". With the help of two others supporting him on each side, Chang Li-chung stood up and took two steps forward. Grasping young Chen's hands and with tears rolling down his cheeks, the veteran miner looked up at Chairman Mao's portrait and shouted over and over: "Long live Chairman Mao!" . . .

NCNA, 24 March 1969

*

. . . While treating members of a production brigade on a snow-capped mountain one day, they found a totally blind Lisu woman holding a portrait of our great leader Chairman Mao and wishing him a long, long life.

This old woman had been a landlord's slave before liberation, and her family had been slaves for generations. Under the wise leadership of Chairman Mao, she had been emancipated after 1949 like the other people of China's minority nationalities. Much as she wanted to see what the great leader Chairman Mao looked like,

thought in command, and we can trample all difficulties and dangers under our feet. Come, let us have our first daily reading and after that we'll begin setting up our station right here".

After he said that, the comrades took out their revolutionary treasure book and began to read aloud on the mountain top surrounded by white clouds: **"What is work? Work is struggle. . . A good comrade is one who is more eager to go where the difficulties are greater"**. Chairman Mao's great teaching illuminated the hearts of the fighters like a powerfully bright beacon light.

Fighter Chang Chuan-fang said: "With Mao Tse-tung thought to guide us, we can use our two hands to make our home here, and we can endure any hardship". Wang Erh-chun was greatly moved and he said: "Fighting in the first line of defence of the fatherland, I am willing to bear all the hardship in the world".

NCNA, 17 November 1969

*

. . Wang was later taken to a certain hospital for treatment. The moment he came out of a coma, he said: "Long live Chairman Mao!" He has never mentioned the pain he has suffered. Instead he speaks quotations from Chairman Mao to gain strength in order to overcome pain. He reads Chairman Mao's works when he is conscious, saying that "only by reciting Chairman Mao's quotations and keeping Chairman Mao in my mind can I feel better and comfortable". He is recovering rapidly from the injuries and will soon be able to work again . . .

Shenyang, Liaoning Provincial Broadcast, 20 September 1969

*

. . . Several days later when he was again conscious the nurse was so happy that she suggested to him that they sing together *The East Is Red*, a song in praise of Chairman Mao.

The east is red, the sun rises,
China has brought forth a Mao Tse-tung . . .

Though his voice faltered and he often stumbled for the words, he finished the song. Every word, every line the hero sang expressed his profound love for our great leader Chairman Mao . . .

Peking Review, No. 47, 17 November 1967

*

. . . [Mai Hsien-teh's] first action when he had partly recovered consciousness but was still unable to speak or move, was to motion to the nurse to read him some quotations from Chairman Mao Tse-tung.

When he had recovered sufficiently to raise the upper-half of his body, despite the shrapnel still in his head and the paralysis of the right side of his body, he would lean against the desk and copy Chairman Mao's quotations for two hours at a time. He made a practice of doing this every day.

Although his memory was seriously impaired, Mai Hsien-teh with great persistence and enthusiasm overcame all difficulties in his studies. Although he still speaks with considerable difficulty, he can now recite rather fluently the three constantly read articles of Chairman Mao, namely, *Serve the People*, *In Memory of Norman Bethune* and *The Foolish Old Man Who Removed the Mountains*, as well as 50 quotations from Chairman Mao. He can also sing 30-odd songs based on the quotations or poems of Chairman Mao . . .

Peking Review, No. 51, 15 December 1967

*

. . . On the journey back to the port, the injured man had great difficulty in breathing. He was very carefully moved on deck, where, as the gunboat proceeded at top speed with waves pounding the deck, 20 naval men, arm in arm, shoulder to shoulder, formed a solid human wall shielding the injured man from the wind and waves. Within the wall, the injured one was fed drop by drop with sustaining liquid while comrades read to him inspiring quotations from Chairman Mao

NCNA, 4 September 1967

OBEYING CHAIRMAN MAO

. . . Mao Tse-tung's thought is universal truth for the whole world and is always the compass for our actions.

Liberation Army Daily, 3 November 1967

*

. . . Chairman Mao is the most outstanding, greatest genius in the world, and his thought is the summing up of the experience of the proletarian struggles in China and abroad and is the unbreakable truth. In implementing Chairman Mao's directives, we must completely disregard the fact whether we understand them or not. The experience of revolutionary struggles tells us that we do not understand many directives of Chairman Mao thoroughly or partly at the beginning, but gradually understand them in the course of implementation, after implementation, or after several years. Therefore, we should implement resolutely Chairman Mao's directives which we understand, as well as those which we temporarily do not understand.

Liberation Army Daily, 13 August 1967

*

. . . Mao Tse-tung's thought is our lifeline. Today importance is not attached to words as criteria whether someone supports or opposes Chairman Mao . . . The hallmark of a person supporting Chairman Mao is that he honestly implements these words: "Chairman Mao gives instructions and I carry them out accordingly; Chairman Mao gives the signal, and I advance". The application of Mao Tse-tung's thought after mastering it is an important manifestation of a comrade's loyalty to Chairman Mao, Mao Tse-tung's thought, and Chairman Mao's revolutionary line. Application has become the basic requirement of any comrade determined to be a proletarian revolutionary.

Wen Hui Pa, 9 December 1967

*

Everything in line with Mao Tse-tung's thought should be supported and followed; everything not in line with Mao Tse-tung's thought should be opposed and resisted. This is a very important principle, which must be resolutely enforced, and must not be violated by the proletarian revolutionaries even after they have seized power.

People's Daily, 26 June 1967

*

. . . The heroes at the construction site studied Chairman Mao's quotations before going to work, as if to accept Chairman Mao's orders; they recited Chairman Mao's quotations while working, so as to follow Chairman Mao's instructions; and after they finished their job they checked their work against Chairman Mao's quotations, as if to receive Chairman Mao's inspection . . .

Liberation Army Daily, 31 October 1967

MERGING SELF WITH CHAIRMAN MAO

... Nien Ssu-wang regained consciousness four days later but he could not remember anyone. Looking at a portrait of Chairman Mao on the wall, a nurse said to the fighter: "Look, there's Chairman Mao!" Nien raised his eyes and fixed his gaze on the portrait. He muttered in a low voice: "Chairman Mao". Then he lost consciousness again ...

Though he relapsed into unconsciousness several more times, Nien Ssu-wang's condition steadily improved and he was soon able to speak and eat. A doctor brought him a sheet of paper and a pencil one morning to see whether he had regained the ability to write, and said to him: "Write a few words, your name if you like". Nien Ssu-wang thought for a while then wrote with great care: "Chairman Mao". But he was still not fully conscious and his memory was poor. He did not recognize his closest comrades from his own squad. Trying to test his memory, his company leader asked: "Ssu-wang, try to think hard and tell me about your family". After thinking for a while the soldier said: "I have Chairman Mao". Asked where his home was he replied: "Peking".

NCNA, 10 October 1967

THE MEMORIAL MEAL

... "It has been customary to eat meat dumplings on the first day of the Spring Festival, but I purposely made steamed corn rolls. I said to the children: 'We take this meal so as not to forget the past sufferings, so as to let you know that our great leader Chairman Mao has brought us today's happiness and so as to make you become good children nurtured by Mao Tse-tung thought' " ...

Peking Radio, 1 June 1969

*

. . . In promoting revolutionization among all the families, the brigade's poor and lower-middle peasants cook a meal every month similar to those they ate in the old society. Over such meals they remind themselves of the misery in which they lived in the old society and think about how they were emancipated. All these activities help them always to bear in mind their hatred for the exploiting classes and raise their consciousness of class struggle and the struggle between the two lines . . .

Peking Radio, 4 April 1970

IMMORTALITY AND REBIRTH IN CHAIRMAN MAO

. . . "My aim in life is to apply Mao Tse-tung's thought, and in death, too, I will die for Mao Tse-tung's thought. Even if I only have one more minute to live, I want to devote it to the Party and the people, to add a stitch, a thread, a line to the pattern of communism drawn by Chairman Mao".

NCNA, 6 December 1967

*

. . . Shen Yu-ying thinks that being able to spread Mao Tse-tung's thought is the highest possible honour. When her friends try to persuade her to rest more and read less so as to give her body a chance, she answers: "I do try to rest but my mind won't be still. There's work to be done and battles to be fought all the time, everywhere . . ."

She was admitted into the Chinese Communist Party in March 1966. She wrote: "Disease has deprived me of my freedom of movement but it can never deprive me of my right to serve the people. So long as my heart beats, I will work wholly and entirely for the people in accordance with the teachings of Chairman Mao Tsetung.

"I will strive to work for the Party for another 10, 20, 30 years . . . If the revolutionary cause can be compared to the Hungching River outside my window, then I am only a drop of water in that river. I believe that as long as I stay in the current of the revolution, my life will go on".

NCNA, 1 February 1967

*

. . . With the help of the P.L.A. medical workers, [barefoot doctor] Hu boldly proceeded to treat the patient. Finally, the patient was able to stand up and began to walk on his own legs. Holding the hands of Hu and the P.L.A. men, the patient said excitedly: "I almost went to my death because of the bourgeois line in health work pushed by Liu Shao-chi. It is only because of the strength of Chairman Mao's line in medical and health work that my life has been saved. I will always be loyal to Chairman Mao".

Hangchow, Chekiang Provincial Broadcast, 8 July 1969

*

. . . Poor herdsman Chao Tzu-ching eventually survived following a successful operation on his brain which was injured during an accident at his work site. Who enabled him to bring back his life from threatening death? It was our great leader Chairman Mao, the red sun in our hearts, the invincible thought of Mao Tse-tung, and Chairman Mao's revolutionary line. These brought him back to life again and gave those who fought for his life the inexhaustible strength and infinite wisdom needed to make such a miracle . . .

Huhehot, Inner Mongolian Regional Broadcast, 8 April 1969

*

. . . The unexpected difficulty did not discourage the medical fighters, who were armed with invincible Mao Tse-tung thought. They decided to brave danger and to try to remove the tumour without affecting the viscera. Thanks to the painstaking efforts made by the medical fighters, the 17-catty tumour was finally removed from little Shu-lan.

Under the enthusiastic care of the medical personnel, little Shu-lan was on the way to recovery. Seeing the quick recovery of his baby, Li Hsi-tasi said with emotion: "It was our great leader Chairman Mao and the Liberation Army led by him who have saved my child and given her a second life".

NCNA, 2 November 1969

*

. . . In the afternoon of the twelfth, a PLA rescue group searching along the northern bank of the lake suddenly saw several small black dots in the distance on the lake. They rushed forward immediately, forgetting their fatigue. At this moment, an aeroplane sent by the proletarian headquarters flew past. With tears of joy in their eyes, the commune members raised their hands and shouted: "Long live Chairman Mao! A long, long life to him!", "Grateful to Chairman Mao! Grateful to the Party Central Committee!" The 24 people set themselves in the form of the Chinese character for "loyalty" to express their infinite loyalty to Chairman Mao, to Mao Tse-tung's thought, and to Chairman Mao's proletarian revolutionary line and their determination to follow Chairman Mao in making revolution all their lives.

When the rescued and the P.L.A. men threw themselves into each other's arms, old poor peasant Ma Yunghai said with deep emotion: "Great are heaven and earth, but greater still is Chairman Mao's goodness; dear are our parents, but dearer still is Chairman Mao to us.

I nearly lost my life at the hands of the Kuomintang gangsters, and Chairman Mao saved me and gave me a second life.

"This time I have been rescued from death again by the P.L.A. men, our kinsmen, who were sent by Chairman Mao. Chairman Mao has given me a third life!" . . .

Peking Radio, 7 March 1969

*

. . . A man of medium build who had been paralysed for four years, Lia Chao-yu, was overwhelmed with excitement when he got on the stage. Waving *Quotations From Chairman Mao Tse-tung*, he jumped with joy and cheered "Long live Chairman Mao!" for at least a minute. He told the audience: "I owe my second life to Chairman Mao. No language in the world can express fully my gratitude to our dear and respected Chairman Mao". He then did a dance in praise of the great leader Chairman Mao. In rhythm with music provided by the band of the art team, his hands went through a series of swift movements and his legs moved quickly and forcefully while his body bent forward and backward. His movements gave no sign that he had once been a paralytic, and that his limbs had been stiff . . .

Peking Radio, 23 March 1969

SOCIALIST PILGRIMAGE

. . . Most college graduates accept re-education very enthusiastically, but some of them do not understand its significance well. To solve this problem, the leading organs of a P.L.A. farm have decided to send these students to "two recalls and three check-ups" classes. They organized the students to visit the Thousand People's Tomb of the child production brigade in the nearby locality where the poor and middle-class peasants were slaughtered in the old society, invited old poor peasants and old ship-yard workers, who suffered great hardship and have deep hatred for the old society, to the company to recall their past sufferings and contrast them with their present happiness, and invited revolutionary veteran cadres to relate their fighting experiences in closely following the great leader Chairman Mao in making revolution.

They then mobilised the students to recall their class sufferings and past national hatred. On the basis of heightening their class consciousness, they have also led the students to recall the history of the victory of the Chinese revolution and to integrate these with their own experience and lessons learned in the proletarian cultural revolution in carrying out the "three check-ups", viz. on their attitude towards Chairman Mao, their attitude towards workers, peasants and soldiers, and their attitude towards receiving re-education. While carrying out the "two recalls and three check-ups", they indignantly condemned Liu Shao-chi's counter-revolutionary revisionist line which has poisoned them, strengthened their confidence in integrating with the workers, peasants and soldiers, and resolved closely to follow the great leader Chairman Mao in carrying the revolution through to the end . . .

Peking Radio, 30 May 1970

THE GLORIFICATION OF CHAIRMAN MAO

"Our most, most beloved and respected great leader Chairman Mao: We, the Red Rebels of Heilungkiang Province who worship you without equal, revere you boundlessly and are forever faithful to you, send to you, the Reddest, Reddest sun in our hearts, the loftiest greeting of the great proletarian cultural revolution . . . Holding tightly to the shiny red treasured books in our hands, we enthusiastically wish you good health as we loudly shout, thousands of times, 'Long live, long live, long live Chairman Mao, the Reddest, Reddest sun in our hearts' . . . We have decided to make the 27th February a permanent day of commemoration which will be celebrated every year as a means of expressing our boundless love, belief in, worship of and loyalty to you . . ."

Harbin Red Rebels' message to Mao on 27 February 1967, to celebrate the 17th anniversary of Mao's visit to Heilungkiang

*

"Chairman Mao, it is your sunshine and dew that has nurtured me and helped me, who used to be a cowherd working for the landlords, to become a proletarian revolutionary fighter with an understanding of service to the people. It is your great and boundlessly brilliant thought that gives me limitless militant strength. Having you and your brilliant thought, the Chinese revolution is bound to be victorious and the world revolution is bound to win success. Communism is bound to emerge throughout the world. The thorough establishment of your absolute authority and the absolute authority of your thought is a historic mission which this great era has entrusted to us, and it is a lifetime militant task for all revolutionary fighters . . .

P.L.A. man in People's Daily, 15 November 1967

*

"Let the seas go dry and the rocks crumble, but our Red revolutionary hearts faithful to Chairman Mao will never change. The heavens may fall and the earth may sink, but we shall forever march forward along Chairman Mao's revolutionary line . . ."

P.L.A. man in People's Daily, 15 November 1967

*

"Respected and beloved Chairman Mao! With tears of joy I pledge myself to engrave on my heart every word and every sentence of yours as I study your works. Nor will I in the least deviate from your instructions when I carry them out. Never for a minute will I stop disseminating your thought. I will not waver but will remain rock-firm, with all my heart and will, in safeguarding your revolutionary line".

P.L.A. man in People's Daily, 15 November 1967

*

"We cheer and sing at this grand festival! Your great thought nourishes us and helps us to mature, and the revolutionary road you have opened us guides us forward to victory! Your concern for us is higher than the mountains and deeper than the seas. Our hearts are brimming over with boundless love for you, faith in you, admiration for you and loyalty towards you! With the deepest feelings we wish you, the bright Red sun in our hearts, a long, long life! A long, long life!"

Message of Tientsin Revolutionary Committee,
NCNA, 7 December 1967

*

. . . [The brigade's] experiences are many, but the most basic experience is that they are boundlessly loyal to Chairman Mao, Mao Tse-tung's thought, and Chairman Mao's proletarian revolutionary line. They say: "Chairman Mao is the very best person in the world. Chairman

Mao's works are the very best books in the world. The fish depends on water and the flower depends on the stalk, and the poor and lower-middle peasants depend on Mao Tse-tung's thought". They hold that they can eat less and sleep less, but they must not read Chairman Mao's works less.

In the struggle between the two classes, two roads, and two lines they have never parted with Chairman Mao's writings, their mouths have always spoken the words of Chairman Mao, their hearts have always been filled with Mao Tse-tung's thought, and their actions have never run counter to Chairman Mao's teachings.

Nanking, Kiangsu Provincial Broadcast, 29 June 1968

*

... "Holding the treasured book in our hands and turning our eyes towards Peking, we, the entire body of commanders and fighters in the Tsinghai Provincial Military District, with tears in our eyes and with deep emotion, loudly cheer: 'Long live Chairman Mao! Long live the Chinese Communist Party!'

"Though the earth is huge and the firmament large, it cannot be compared with the great love of the Party! Chairman Mao is dearer to us than our fathers and mothers! . . ."

Sining, Tsinghai Provincial Broadcast, 2 April 1969

*

"Most respected and beloved great leader Chairman Mao: The red sun illuminates the world; the spring thunder shakes the earth. The Party's Ninth National Congress, expected night and day by the people of all nationalities in Sinkiang, has successfully opened under your personal guidance. This is the most brilliant event in the history of the international communist movement. All of Sinkiang is resounding with cheers following the circulation of the tidings on the opening of the Party's

Ninth National Congress. The people of all nationalities in the countryside, as well as in the cities, in the grasslands, and in the frontier sentry posts, have jubilantly sung with grateful tears in their eyes. Their red hearts are facing the capital of Peking and they are singing in praise of you—the Red sun shining most brightly in their hearts. They have repeatedly shouted great victory for your brilliant thought and for your revolutionary line and have heartily wished a long life, a long, long life to you . . .

"Chairman Mao: On the occasion of this festive day, the people of all nationalities in Sinkiang solemnly pledge to you that by taking Vice Chairman Lin as a brilliant example they are determined to study your writings forever, follow your teachings, act in accordance with your instructions, and use your brilliant thought to guide every second of their lives and to unify thinking, policies, plans, command and actions. They will defend until death your revolutionary line. The seas may dry up and the rocks may decay, but their loyalty to you will never change. The sky may fall and the earth may collapse, but they will forever closely follow you . . ."

> *Urumchi, Sinkiang Regional Broadcast, Message of Salute to Chairman Mao from the 2 April Urumchi rally celebrating the Party Congress opening, 3 April* 1969

*

. . . The Company's deputy political instructor was checking through the dormitory at midnight one night after the soldiers had seen the film of Mao's reception of Red Guards, and observed the platoon's leader, Li Wen-hung, still smiling and murmuring in his sleep "Chairman Mao, Chairman Mao". The instructor was so moved that he wrote a poem about it.

> *NCNA*, 8 December 1967

Appendix A

The "Three Constantly Read Articles"

In Memory of Norman Bethune

The surgeon Norman Bethune was a member of the Canadian Communist Party. After working at the front during the Spanish Civil War he headed a medical team to China, reaching Yenan in the spring of 1938. He contracted blood poisoning while operating on wounded soldiers and died on 12 November 1939. Mao's article was written just over a month later—21 December 1939.

Comrade Norman Bethune, a member of the Communist Party of Canada, was around 50 when he was sent by the Communist Parties of Canada and the United States to China; he made light of travelling thousands of miles to help us in our War of Resistance against Japan. He arrived in Yenan in the spring of last year, went to work in the Wutai Mountains, and to our great sorrow died a martyr at his post. What kind of spirit is this that makes a foreigner selflessly adopt the cause of the Chinese people's liberation as his own? It is the spirit of internationalism, the spirit of communism, from which every Chinese Communist must learn. Leninism teaches that the world revolution can only succeed if the proletariat of the capitalist countries supports the struggle for liberation of the colonial and semi-colonial peoples and if the proletariat of the colonies and semi-colonies supports that of the proletariat of the capitalist countries. Comrade Bethune put this Leninist line into practice. We Chinese Communists must also follow this line in our practice. We must unite with the proletariat of all the capitalist countries, with the proletariat of Japan, Britain, the United States, Germany, Italy and all other capitalist countries, for this is the only way to overthrow imperialism, to liberate our nation and people and to liberate the other nations and peoples of the world. This is our internationalism, the internationalism with which we oppose both narrow nationalism and narrow patriotism.

Comrade Bethune's spirit, his utter devotion to others without any thought of self, was shown in his great sense of responsibility in his work and his great warm-heartedness towards all comrades and the people. Every Communist must learn from him. There are not a few people who are irresponsible in their work, preferring the light and shirking the heavy, passing the burdensome tasks on to others and choosing the easy ones for themselves. At every turn they think of themselves before others. When they make some small contribution, they swell with pride and brag about it for fear that others will not know. They feel no warmth towards comrades and the people but are cold, indifferent and apathetic. In truth such people are not Communists, or at least cannot be counted as devoted Communists. No one who returned from the front failed to express admiration for Bethune whenever his name was mentioned, and none remained unmoved by his spirit. In the Shansi-Chahar-Hopei border area, no soldier or civilian was unmoved who had been treated by Dr. Bethune or had seen how he worked. Every Communist must learn this true communist spirit from Comrade Bethune.

Comrade Bethune was a doctor, the art of healing was his profession and he was constantly perfecting his skill, which stood very high in the Eighth Route Army's medical service. His example is an excellent lesson for those people who wish to change their work the moment they see something different and for those who despise technical work as of no consequence or as promising no future.

Comrade Bethune and I met only once. Afterwards he wrote me many letters. But I was busy, and I wrote him only one letter and do not know if he ever received it. I am deeply grieved over his death. Now we are all commemorating him, which shows how profoundly his spirit inspires everyone. We must all learn the spirit of absolute selflessness from him. With this spirit everyone can be very useful to the people. A man's ability may be great or small, but if he has this spirit, he is already noble-minded and pure, a man of moral integrity and above vulgar interests, a man who is of value to the people.

SERVE THE PEOPLE

This speech was delivered by Mao at a memorial meeting for Chang Szu-teh, held by departments under the CCP Central Committee in Yenan, 8 September 1944. Chang, a member of the Guards Regiment of the CCP Central Committee, had been killed three days previously when a charcoal kiln in which he was working suddenly collapsed.

Our Communist Party and the Eighth Route and New Fourth Armies led by our Party are battalions of the revolution. These battalions of ours are wholly dedicated to the liberation of the people and work entirely in the people's interests. Comrade Chang Szu-teh was in the ranks of these battalions.

All men must die, but death can vary in its significance. The ancient Chinese writer Szuma Chien said, "Though death befalls all men alike, it may be heavier than Mount Tai or lighter than a feather". To die for the people is heavier than Mount Tai, but to work for the fascists and die for the exploiters and oppressors is lighter than a feather. Comrade Chang Szu-teh died for the people, and his death is indeed heavier than Mount Tai.

If we have shortcomings, we are not afraid to have them pointed out and criticized, because we serve the people. Anyone, no matter who, may point out our shortcomings. If he is right, we will correct them. If what he proposes will benefit the people, we will act upon it. The idea of "better troops and simpler administration" was put forward by Li Ting-ming, who is not a Communist. He made a good suggestion which is of benefit to the people, and we have adopted it. If, in the interests of the people, we persist in doing what is right and correct what is wrong, our ranks will surely thrive.

We hail from all corners of the country and have joined together for a common revolutionary objective. And we need the vast majority of the people with us on the road to this objective. Today, we already lead base areas with a population of 91 million, but this is not enough; to liberate the whole nation more are needed. In times of difficulty we must not lose sight of our achievements, must see the bright future and must pluck up our courage. The Chinese people are suffering; it is our duty to save them and we must exert ourselves in struggle. Wherever there is struggle there is sacrifice, and death is a common occurrence. But we have the interests of the people and the sufferings of the great majority at heart, and when we die for the people it is a worthy death. Nevertheless, we should do out best to avoid unnecessary sacrifices. Our cadres must show concern for every soldier, and all people in the revolutionary ranks must care for each other, must love and help each other.

From now on, when anyone in our ranks who has done some useful work dies, be he soldier or cook, we should have a funeral ceremony and a memorial meeting in his honour. This should become the rule. And it should be introduced among the people as well. When someone dies in a village, let a memorial meeting be held. In this way we express our mourning for the dead and unite all the people.

THE FOOLISH OLD MAN
WHO REMOVED THE MOUNTAINS

This was Mao Tse-tung's concluding speech at the Seventh National Congress of the Communist Party of China, 11 June 1945.

We have had a very successful congress. We have done three things. First, we have decided on the line of our Party, which is boldly to mobilize the masses and expand the people's forces so that, under the leadership of our Party, they will defeat the Japanese aggressors, liberate the whole people and build a new-democratic China. Second, we have adopted the new Party Constitution. Third, we have elected the leading body of the Party – the Central Committee. Henceforth our task is to lead the whole membership in carrying out the Party line. Ours has been a congress of victory, a congress of unity. The delegates have made excellent comments on the three reports. Many comrades have undertaken self-criticism and, setting out with unity as the objective, have arrived at unity through self-criticism. This congress is a model of unity, of self-criticism and of inner-Party democracy.

When the congress closes, many comrades will be leaving for their posts and the various war fronts. Comrades, wherever you go, you should propagate the line of the congress and, through the members of the Party, explain it to the broad masses.

Our aim in propagating the line of the congress is to build up the confidence of the whole Party and the entire people in the certain triumph of the revolution. We must first raise the political consciousness of the vanguard so that, resolute and unafraid of sacrifice, they will surmount every difficulty to win victory. But this is not enough; we must also arouse the political consciousness of the entire people so that they may willingly and gladly fight together with us for victory. We should fire the whole people with the conviction that China belongs not the to reactionaries but to the Chinese people. There is an ancient Chinese fable called "The Foolish Old Man Who Removed the Mountains". It tells of an old man who lived in northern China long, long ago and was known as the Foolish Old Man of North Mountain. His house faced south and beyond his doorway stood the two great peaks, Taihang and Wangwu, obstructing the way. He called his sons, and hoe in hand they began to dig up these mountains with great determination. Another greybread known as the Wise Old Man, saw them and said derisively, "How silly of you to do this! It is quite impossible for you few to dig up these two huge mountains". The Foolish Old Man replied, "When I die, my sons will carry on; when they die, there will be my grandsons, and then their sons and grandsons, and so on to infinity. High as they are, the mountains cannot grow any higher and with every bit we dig, they will be that much lower. Why can't we clear them away?" Having refuted the Wise Old Man's wrong view, he went on digging every day, unshaken in his conviction. God was moved by this, and he sent down two angels, who carried the mountains away on their backs. Today, two big mountains lie like a dead weight on the Chinese people. One is imperialism, the other is feudalism. The Chinese Communist Party has long made up its mind to dig them up. We must persevere and work unceasingly, and we, too, will touch God's heart. Our God is none other than the masses of the Chinese people. If they stand up and dig together with us, why can't these two mountains be cleared away?

Yesterday, in a talk with two Americans who were leaving for the United States, I said that the U.S. government was trying to undermine us and this would not be permitted. We oppose the U.S. government's policy of supporting Chiang Kai-shek against the Communists. But we must draw a distinction, firstly, between the people of the United States and their government and, secondly, within the U.S. government between the policy-makers and their subordinates. I said to these two Americans, "Tell the policy-makers in your government that we forbid you Americans to enter the Liberated Areas because your policy is to support Chiang Kai-shek against the Communists, and we have to be on our guard. You can come to the Liberated Areas if your purpose is to fight Japan, but there must first be an agreement. We will not permit you to nose around everywhere. Since Patrick J. Hurley has publicly declared against co-operation with the Chinese Communist Party, why do you still want to come and prowl around in our Liberated Areas?"

The U.S. government's policy of supporting Chiang Kai-shek against the Communists shows the brazenness of the U.S. reactionaries. But all the scheming of the reactionaries, whether Chinese or foreign, to prevent the Chinese people from achieving victory is doomed to failure. The democratic forces are the main current in the world today, while reaction is only a counter-current. The reactionary counter-current is trying to swamp the main current of national independence and people's democracy, but it can never become the main current. Today, there are still three major contradictions in the old world, as Stalin pointed out long ago: first, the contradiction between the proletariat and the bourgeoisie in the imperialist countries; second, the contradiction between the various imperialist powers; and third, the contradiction between the colonial and semi-colonial countries and the imperialist metropolitan countries. Not only do these three contradictions continue to exist but they are becoming more acute and widespread. Because of their existence and growth, the time will come when the reactionary anti-Soviet, anti-Communist and anti-democratic counter-current still in exitence today will be swept away.

At this moment two congresses are being held in China, the Sixth National Congress of the Kuomintang and the Seventh National Congress of the Communist Party. They have completely different aims: the aim of one is to liquidate the Communist Party and all the other democratic forces in China and thus to plunge China into darkness; the aim of the other is to overthrow Japanese imperialism and its lackeys, the Chinese feudal forces, and build a new-democratic China and thus to lead China to light. These two lines are in conflict with each other. We firmly believe that, led by the Chinese Communist Party and guided by the line of its Seventh Congress, the Chinese people will achieve complete victory, while the Kuomintang's counter-revolutionary line will inevitably fail.

Appendix B

A SOVIET VIEW OF THE
CULT OF MAO TSE-TUNG

THE MAKING OF AN IDOL

M. Yakovlev

. . . The Mao cult lies like a heavy yoke around the neck of social, political and economic life in China today. The Peking leadership tries to fit it to the Procrustean bed of the so-called "thoughts of Mao Tse-tung".

Having unleashed the "cultural revolution", Mao and his group then proceeded to initiate the organizational destruction of the C.C.P. and the removal from leadership of all "heretics" in the Party and government cadres. At the same time the "cultural revolution", as the Chinese leaders have put it, is designed to abolish completely the "old ideology" and implant a new one. The *Chiehfang Chunpao*, organ of the Chief Political Department of the Chinese P.L.A., which sets the tune in political life in China today, has stated: "We must carry out a revolution against the old ideology and replace it with the new ideology of the thought of Mao Tse-tung".

Monopoly of Thought

Mao has been invested with the halo of "genius", "sagacity" and "infallibility". His thought is represented as the "food", "weapon", "compass" and "beacon" of the Chinese people. The Chinese press has ascribed to Mao the monopoly in drafting Party and state policy throughout the entire history of the C.C.P. and P.R.C. It says that "the directives and documents of the Party and supreme organs are but concretisations of the thought of Mao Tse-tung". The writings of Mao are termed the "concentrated expression of the Chinese people's entire age-old heritage". His pronouncements, and quotations from Mao's articles are officially styled "the supreme injunctions of the great leader".

Idolatry of one man is withering the minds of millions of Chinese who are being deprived of the urge to think, as the "great leader" thinks for them. It has done and is continuing to do irreparable material damage to the national economy and has discredited the P.R.C.'s international prestige as a socialist state. Examples are afforded by the "great leap forward" in industry and farming in 1958-59 and the present "cultural revolution".

At the time of the foundation of the people's communes, Mao suggested splitting up the country's arable land into three parts, one for cereals, industrial crops and vegetables, the other for gardens and orchards, and the third for forests. The very next year this resulted in a drastic decline in the sown area. Equally dangerous were the two other agricultural measures the "great helmsman" also suggested.

The "eight-character constitution" – or eight rules of farming– advise the Chinese peasants to do "deep ploughing" down to one metre and more. A legion of peasants surged out onto the fields and dug up the earth with spades, thus impairing soil structure and wasting the country's stock of fertilizer and manure, which was already paltry enough. Far from increasing, crop yields went down.

A sweeping irrigation programme was initiated in the countryside, with Mao in the role of expert. However, construction went ahead without the application of any of the techniques of hydraulic engine-ering and even contrary to traditional farming experience. Reser-voirs were constructed in every gully and ravine without any thought given as to how they were going to raise the water and channel it to the fields. During the rains these arrangements not infrequently produced terrible disasters. One instance of this ignorance, the product of Mao's whims, is the Shihsanling reservoir outside Peking. At short order millions of Peking residents and P.L.A. men built this reservoir, while the press raved about the "paradise" being created around it. Mao himself came along with his retinue. However, the water collected in the reservoir soon seeped out and now this bog of mud lies there, a monument to the wilful stupidity of the "great helmsman".

Or take the "nation-wide movement for steel" and the damage it did to the country. Factory and office workers, peasants and school children without the slightest notion of metallurgy were enlisted. Central newspapers eulogized the pupils of Peking's Secondary School No. 8 who "having learned the trades" of builders and metallurgists made the rounds of enterprises in the capital to teach the workers how to build "blast furnaces". Millions of fires were lit throughout the country. Metal was melted everywhere – at farms, schools, textile mills and offices. About 100 million peasants and factory and office workers were taken away from their immediate jobs and made to smelt metal or bring up ore and coal to the "blast furnaces". In only a few months of 1958 the two million home-made metal furnaces gobbled up scores of millions of tons of iron ore and coal to yield scattered piles of absolutely useless low-grade metal.

New Religion

After the dire upheavals brought about by the "great leap" and the people's communes, Mao and his entourage, fearful that their economic ignorance would be exposed, and seeking to escape the responsibility for the failure experienced over the years of so-called economic "adjustment", started anew to inflate the Mao cult. It was dinned into Chinese heads that Mao was "infallible" and that his pernicious policies and directives were "absolutely right". Mao and his group blamed the rank-and-file for all the blunders perpetrated in economic policies at home, alleging that they had misunderstood "the leader's brilliant injunctions" and had wrongly implemented them. The writings of Mao and his "thought" are represented as the "universal golden key" to all major and minor issues in work and life.

The country's entire gigantic propaganda machine has been ordered to compel old and young to study the works of the "great helmsman". For many years now the entire Chinese press has been crammed with frenzied calls to "learn from Mao Tse-tung". Hundreds of thousands of study-circles and groups have been organized. Even families are made to form such groups.

The press exhorts people to read Mao's writings not just once or several times but countless numbers of times, to learn them by heart like the canons of Confucius. They are trying to get the ordinary Chinese to learn the writings of Mao by rote "daily, everywhere, during work and leisure, nursing and cooking, in trains and trams and at night – in the glow of street lamps or family hearths should there not be enough light".

So that no other literature – political, fiction or scientific – should be read during the "cultural revolution", it was declared "revisionist" throughout, virtually banned and withdrawn by the "Red Guards" from shops and private libraries or locked up in library bookcases.

In recent months a clamorous new campaign has been launched to assert the "absolute authority" of Mao and his "thought" in China. The propaganda machine demands that all state institutions be transformed into departments of the "thought of Mao Tse-tung" and the entire country into a "school of the thought of Mao Tse-tung". Early this year Peking "Red Guards" even urged turning lunatic asylums into "homes of the thought of Mao Tse-tung for the mad". The newspaper *Shoutu Hungweiping*[1] said, for instance: "We call on the revolutionary personnel of the country's asylums to establish completely red hospitals guided by the great red banner of the thought of Mao Tse-tung, so that the lunatic asylums become an implement of the dictatorship of the proletariat and fully and completely serve the people. Comrades, by joint effort let us kindle a powerful revolutionary flame in the psychiatric hospitals of the entire country!"

Neck Tag

Printing shops are competing for the advance fulfilment of plans for the publication of Mao's "works" while the propaganda machine seeks to have these books in every home. Late last year the *Fukien Jihpao* said that in the Chouning region in Fukien Province, for 20,000 homes there were a total of 160,000 volumes of Mao's writings, that is nearly eight volumes per home. A four-volume *Selected Writings of Mao Tse-tung* has been published. To compel people to buy these books the press describes countless instances of the "enthusiasm" of would-be purchasers. Thus, the self-same *Fukien Jihpao* reported that 60-year-old Huang Sung-hsi, a poor farmer of the Changyuan production brigade, "walked 140 li[2] from home to buy the books of Chairman Mao though he himself could not read a single character". However, he asked others to read these writings, remembering them by heart and drawing pictures of what he could not remember. In this way, according to the paper, he learned three of Mao's articles by heart.

In the process of the "cultural revolution" placards and posters with quotations from Mao's articles have blotted out everything else in town and country. Orders were issued to put a tag with a quotation on every bicycle, even if the cyclist could not read. Quotations from Mao were hung on the necks of donkeys and on barrels of night-soil. Household utensils, stationery and other manufactured goods are produced only with quotations.

A campaign was started in the country late last year to turn China into a "red ocean". Bright red paint was splashed on housewalls and fences in town and country, with Mao quotations inscribed across them. In Peking and other cities today one can see completely red streets that are peppered with his quotations.

These quotations have been collected into a separate booklet which is published in millions of copies. Not a single event, film

[1] *Psychiartic Hospitals to Rebel Against the Old Type of Lunatic [Asylums].*
[2] One'li' is km. 0.5.

showing, rally or meeting starts off without the recitation of it in chorus. It is recited for hours on end by passengers in buses, trolley-buses, trains and aircraft. There is really no other book in China today. Its reading and recitation starts without any introductory explanation. Chinese propagandists are out to get the ordinary Chinese to accept the "leader's" pronouncements without any further thought or reflection.

These quotations are not only read or recited, they have been set to music and are presented choreographically. The newspapers regularly print such "songs", and they are taught by radio.

Mao's name is repeated thousands of times daily over the radio and in the press. In cinemas one sees nothing but Mao in close-up against the background of a faceless mass of "Red Guards" and revolutionary rebels, because the only films shown are those about Mao and his meetings with the "Red Guards". Streets and squares in town and country are hung with pictures of the "leader". They are displayed in every shop window, in buses, trolleybuses and cabs, in every policeman's shelter and over the entrance of nearly every house and office. A plaster or marble effigy of the "helmsman" is to be found in nearly every public place. In Chinghai Province printers were given the task of producing 10 portraits for every person living in the province.

Idolatry

The "thoughts of Mao Tse-tung" have been proclaimed, to all practical intents, to be the new religion of the Chinese people, and Mao himself has been deified. In fact Mao's deification has surpassed everything in Oriental history ever written about the sumptuous reigns of "god's viceroys on earth". Like a modern Great Mogul he now appears to the people but does not speak, merely giving his blessing with a hand raised in greeting. Newspapers, posters and other printed matter depict Mao in a halo of sunbeams, while he himself is compared to the celestial luminary and is styled "the Reddest of Red suns". The military paper *Tsehgang Jihpao* thus described Mao's visit to a warship: "Chairman Mao emerged from the cabin . . . Two red suns, one in the heavens, the other among people, shone forth with rays some 10,000 changs long". The *Fukien Jihpao* went still further in its adulation. "The power of Chairman Mao's writings", it said, "is much greater than that of the elements of heaven and earth".

In the Chinese home, portraits and busts of the new "god" now adorn the place where earlier, that pillar of Confucianism, the effigies of deities and tablets with the names of one's ancestors were preserved. "Where before there stood the three gods of happiness, fortune and longevity", the Shanghai paper *Tsehfang Jihpao* wrote, describing the home of a Chiangnan shipyards worker in Shanghai, "today hangs the picture of Chairman Mao in a yard-high frame".

His picture is worshipped in prayer as if an icon, and people go to genuflect before sculptural effigies of Mao. Describing the new system introduced at educational establishments, one Peking "Red Guard" newspaper said that every pupil upon entering school bowed thrice before Mao's picture or bust. At marriage ceremonies bride and groom do the same. One provincial Chinese paper reported that on holidays peasants install a picture of Mao in the middle of the village and genuflect before it. Peasants go out to the fields carrying Mao's pictures. Sometimes the field where they may be working will be fenced off with Mao's pictures. Tibetan peasants have placed next to effigies of Buddha large and small busts of Mao Tse-tung and sanctified towels are presented as a votive offering in the same way as to Buddha.

In the streets and thoroughfares of Chinese cities "Red Guards" and revolutionary rebels carry chest-high, like icons, the portrait of Mao Tse-tung. Soldiers marching in rank do the same. One may sometimes see the men of a whole military unit marching with Mao's pictures, some even carrying two, one in their hands and another in a frame suspended from the neck.

In their zealous exultation of Mao, Chinese propagandists lose all sense of proportion. The *Jenmin Jihpao* once featured an article by Kuo Mo-jo, President of the Chinese Academy of Sciences, about the "love and affection" foreigners bear for Mao. With absolute seriousness, this "scholar" writes: "During one international forum in Peking Mao Tse-tung received some of the participants and gave one of them his hand. This fortunate man shared his delight with his colleagues who advised him to bathe his hands in a large basin so that the others too could rinse their hands in the same water".

Paradoxes of the Cult

The Chinese is taught to thank Mao for everything, for the fact that he lives, eats and drinks, for his daily bowl of rice and cup of tea and even for a service rendered by someone else. Replying to thanks expressed by a patron for returning a forgotten parcel a restaurant waiter answered: "It's not me you should thank but Chairman Mao". Army nurse Chu Yu-lan, when thanked by an old lady, Chang Sheng-en, for curing her constipation, said: "If there's anyone you'd like to thank, thank Chairman Mao". This edifying story was featured in the Young Pioneer paper *Chungkuo Shaopao*.

The Chinese is compelled to deny himself even the minimum independent thought or action, because all this is regarded as contamination with "egoism" and "revisionism", as "degeneration", as setting foot on the "capitalist road".

Worship of Mao is cultivated by the open use of force. To suppress all protest, indignation and doubt, a barrack-type discipline is being enforced throughout the country. The civilian population are today told to live according to army regulations and to emulate the army which "obeys orders quickly, strictly, with determination, without remonstrance and haggling" and "does what it is told to do". The official press, that is "Red Guard" newspapers, slogans and posters, say outright that everyone criticising Mao will be ruthlessly suppressed.

Today the Chinese, to avoid being suspect, uses a Mao badge or the book of his quotations for protection. Even housewives put this loyal "charm" in their string bags when going off to the market.

The editorial staffs of Chinese newspapers, magazines and radio, along with a legion of propagandists, have contributed thousands upon thousands of items, articles and stories to show how Mao's writings help people in their none too easy life to tackle diverse problems, big and small, and drum away day after day that these writings possess an incomparable, magic power. Any event, anything in ordinary life, let alone things out of the ordinary, are invariably associated with the name of Mao, his "thought", his "supreme injunctions".

Chinese propagandists claim that any person who brings something found to the lost property office, helps an elderly man to get into a bus, points out the way to someone, or saves a drowning child, does this only because he is "a good pupil of Chairman Mao" and has possessed himself of his "thought". The Army paper *Tsehfangchum pao* tells the story of the reform of an army hospital woman orderly who was ashamed of her job before, cold-shouldered the patients and paid no heed to a blocked toilet. However, having read one night for six times in succession Mao's article *Serve the People*, she "seemed to discard this heavy burden" and "the very next day before dawn rushed off to the hospital to tidy up the toilet". The Hsinhua news agency reported that the recent shooting down of an American U-2 spy plane by Chinese anti-aircraft forces had happened only because the commanders of airforce unit N had "officered the battle with the help of quotations from the writings of

Mao Tse-tung".

Finally one more sample from a host that could be given about the application of Mao's writings. It is also taken from the Chinese press. The farm personnel of military unit N decided to breed ducks. They purchased some ducklings, but, when about to float them in the pond, started arguing as to whether the little things could swim or not. Some said they could, others that they couldn't. To settle the argument, they invoked Mao's article *On Practice*. From it they learned that theory is tested in practice. So they decided to put the ducklings in the pond and the ducklings began to swim. The writer of the article sums up: it is in this way that the "study of the works of Chairman Mao, closely linked to life," helps to solve practical problems.

Despite the wholesale inflation of the Mao cult, developments in the "cultural revolution" show that the present leadership of Peking is failing to force the life of the Chinese people into the straitjacket of propaganda and make them live according to army rules and regulations. The same developments in the "cultural revolution" likewise show that both at the top and the bottom of the social ladder a reassessment of Mao's "grandeur" and "infallibility" is taking place and that the more conscientious sections of Chinese society are starting to realize the tragedy and ugliness of the personality cult, which is being inflated by the new-style zealots of great-khan chauvinism for their own ends.

Za Rubezhom No. 5, 1968

Glossary

Big Character posters Propaganda posters written in big characters, stuck on walls and boards.

Capitalist roaders Anyone who, by Maoist standards, uses or advocates capitalist methods. Followers of Liu Shao-chi.

China's Khrushchev Veiled reference to Liu Shao-chi in the early stages of the cultural revolution.

Contending and blooming These two words stand for the old phrase "one hundred schools of thought contend, and one hundred flowers bloom". A campaign of "letting different schools of thought contend (freely air views on academic theories) and hundred flowers bloom (freely create arts, especially plays and dramas)" was launched towards the end of 1956 and in the first part of 1957. Many people, especially members of the so-called democratic parties, thought that they were given freedom to air their views and began to criticise the policies of the Chinese Communist Party. As a result, they were attacked and downgraded by the Party.

Economism The practice of using wage increases and other material benefits to undermine the revolutionary zeal of the working people and lure them away from the Maoist line. The term has its origins in the early history of the Russian Social Democratic Party.

Five-anti campaign A campaign, in 1951 and 1952, directed against bribery, tax evasion, fraud, theft of state property and leakage of economic secrets. It furnished the background to public trials and mass executions.

Five category elements	These are landlords, rich peasants, counter-revolutionaries, bad elements and rightists.
Five-good commune member	A five-good member must be good in: (*a*) politics and ideology; (*b*) the three-eight working style; (*c*) fulfilling tasks; (*d*) production techniques, grasping scientific experiments and technical innovations and (*e*) patriotic sanitation.
Four freedoms	The freedom to engage in usury, to hire labour, to sell land and to run private enterprises, a slogan alleged to have been advanced by Liu Shao-chi during the land reform period.
Four-good units (of the P.L.A.)	Must be good in: (*a*) politics and ideology, putting Mao's thought in command; (*b*) the three-eight working style; (*c*) fulfilling tasks and (*d*) the management of daily life, paying attention to coordinating labour, rest and grasping public health and cultural work.
Four-olds	Old ideas, old culture, old customs and old habits. In the cultural revolution, teenage students were organized for the first time in August 1966, as Red Guards to eradicate the "four-olds" of the exploiting classes.
Ghosts and monsters	All "ugly beings" who oppose the Chinese Communist Party and the thought of Mao Tse-tung.
Great Leap Forward	The term is used to describe the ambitious development of production in the years 1956, 1957 and 1958 in the form of a leap forward.
Mao Tse-tung's thought v. Mao Tse-tung thought	In April 1969, at the 9th Congress of the C.C.P., Mao Tse-tung thought was enshrined in the Chinese Party's Constitution, and thereafter generally used, as a generic term, on a par with Marxism and Leninism.
One divides into two	This refers to the Marxist method of dialectical analysis. According to Chinese communist interpretation it means that one must look

at a person or work from two sides: the good features and the defects. Struggle of one against the other brings about progress in a person and uninterrupted development of work.

P.L.A: People's Liberation Army.

Rectification A campaign carried out by the Party to enhance the people's consciousness of communism. Its principal method is that of criticism and self-criticism, with preference for small discussion groups and personal interviews.

Red pair One who is "red" assisting another who is not. "Red" denotes political reliability.

Repudiation A critical rejection of old policies, values and principles.

Self-cultivation Refers to three of Liu Shao-chi's articles in *How to be a Good Communist*. Since Liu Shao-chi's fall, "self-cultivation" has been used as a slogan to attack individualism and selfishness and to denounce Liu's alleged refusal to make a clear theoretical stand supporting the dictatorship of the proletariat.

Struggle-criticism-transformation The three stages of rectification ending in the remoulding of self and the acquisition of a correct political outlook.

Sugar-coated bullets Methods used to divert the people from the revolutionary line, such as monetary incentives.

Tachai Situated at the foot of the poverty-stricken Tiger Head Hills of the Taihang Mountains in northern China, Tachai is a model production brigade of the Tachai People's commune. It consists of 83 households with a population of 380 and owns 796 *mou* of arable land (1 mou equals about one-sixth of an acre).

GLOSSARY

Tachai spirit	The spirit of self-reliance. It is claimed that, by dogged effort, the peasants of Tachai transformed, between 1958 and 1968, their barren hills into fertile terraces.
Three-anti campaign	A campaign in 1951 against corruption, waste and bureaucracy.
Three capitulations and one abolition	The phrase is used to sum up crimes committed by Lui Shao-chi in China's external policies. Liu is here accused of capitulating to the imperialists, to the Soviet revisionists and to foreign reactionaries. He is also alleged to have sought to abolish the anti-imperialistic struggle of the suppressed peoples of the world.
Three constantly read articles	See Appendix A.
Three-eight working style	The three phrases and eight characters written by Mao Tse-tung to describe the working style that officers and men of the P.L.A. were exhorted to adopt. These are: correct political direction, a simple and arduous working style and flexible strategy and tactics. The eight characters mean: unity, alertness, earnestness, liveliness. The "three-eight" working style is an important part of Mao Tse-tung's military thinking, a concentrated expression of the nature of the people's army and the standard for its training and combat.
Three freedoms and one contract	The three freedoms refer to the extension of plots of land for private production, free markets and increase of private enterprises. One contract means allowing each household to assume a contractual obligation towards the state for producing a fixed quantity of grain.
Two lines	Those of capitalism and socialism.